CW00350128

PENNINE PIONEER
the story of
THE ROCHDALE CANAL

PENNINE PIONEER

the story of

THE ROCHDALE CANAL

KEITH GIBSON

TEMPUS

Frontispiece: Not so long ago the canal in central Manchester was nearly derelict and the canalside deserted. How different it is in this busy scene at Canal Street today. Chorlton Street Lock (No.86) is in the background. (Courtesy of Marketing Manchester)

First published 2004

Tempus Publishing Ltd
The Mill, Brimscombe Port
Stroud, Gloucestershire GL5 2QG
www.tempus-publishing.com

© Keith Gibson, 2004

The right of Keith Gibson to be identified as the Author
of this work has been asserted by him in accordance with the
Copyrights, Designs and Patents Act 1988.

All rights reserved. No part of this book may be reprinted
or reproduced or utilised in any form or by any electronic,
mechanical or other means, now known or hereafter invented,
including photocopying and recording, or in any information
storage or retrieval system, without the permission in writing
from the Publishers.

British Library Cataloguing in Publication Data.
A catalogue record for this book is available from the British Library.

ISBN 0 7524 3266 4

Typesetting and origination by Tempus Publishing.
Printed and bound in Great Britain.

CONTENTS

ACKNOWLEDGEMENTS

I could not have written this book without a great deal of help. My main purpose was to tell the story of the restoration of the canal so the early chapters depend very much on the research of others as set out in the Bibliography. I gleaned the basic story of restoration from my own memories and from articles in the waterways press but especially from lengthy discussions with Brian Holden, the secretary of the Rochdale Canal Society.

I was able to put meat on the bones of this story by information provided by local authority and British Waterways' officers. In particular I must thank Adrian Rose, Brendan Mowforth, Dick Booth and Nigel Lord (Calderdale MBC), Andy Swaby, Adrian Montgomery, Chris Flintoff and David Lloyd (Rochdale MBC), John Billington, Graham Pointon and John Bland (Oldham MBC), Nigel Bodman (Manchester City Council) and Keith Paylor (British Waterways). Adrian Rose let me borrow his files. Dick Booth lent me his diaries. John Billington, Andy Swaby and Keith Paylor all provided notes. Adrian Rose, Brendan Mowforth and John Billington were kind enough to wade through an early draft and pick up obvious errors. Ronald Rees, the project officer for the Millennium bid, described the tortuous process of satisfying the funding agencies. Many other people helped. I must especially mention Mark Andrew, Councillor Allen Brett, Dave Fletcher, Michael Handford, Andrew Hardwick, Keith Parry, Nigel Stevens and John Sully for their useful information and comments. Dave Marsland, a former chairman of the Canal Society, dredged his memories of the M60 Public Inquiry. At the Cheshire Record Office and Chester Diocesan Record Office, Katie Goodrum searched out details of Archdeacon George Travis. Jean Jones of Rochdale Library provided information on old local histories. Anthony Burton kindly allowed me to quote from his book *The Great Days of the Canals*.

Discovering suitable illustrations was fascinating, though at times frustrating, and I am grateful for the help I have been given in finding material and the permissions given to reproduce illustrations. I must thank John Billington (Oldham MBC), Dick Booth (Calderdale MBC), David Evans (the editor of the Rochdale Canal Society newsletter), John and Margaret Fletcher, my wife,

Kathryn, Keith Noble, Adrian Rose (Calderdale MBC), Ron Tinker (the chairman of the Rochdale Canal Society) and Robin Witter for allowing me to use their photographs. David kindly spent many hours searching through his extensive collection of negatives and printing the images I wanted. Robin bravely mounted a tall stepladder in Chester Cathedral. Jack Kershaw pointed me in the direction of historic photographs. Tony Hurst kindly searched through historic Rochdale Canal Company material at the Boat Museum and selected possible images; archivist Nicola Samuel efficiently and rapidly reproduced those I was able to use. Graham Pearson, secretary of the Littleborough Historical Society, enthusiastically searched the society's archives for suitable illustrations and arranged the provision of copies. Lynn Pegler kindly found and allowed me to use suitable images from British Waterways' collection. Tracey Walker, of Manchester Art Gallery, Lisa Ashurst, of Urban Splash and Alan Bellwood, of Marketing Manchester found just the appropriate images to illustrate the benefits of the canal to Manchester in the early 1800s and today.

The final text benefited enormously from the attention to detail of my editors Wendy Tse and Nicola Sweet.

Although the help and advice of many people was essential in writing the book, any errors are likely to be of my making.

Keith Gibson
Holmfirth 2004

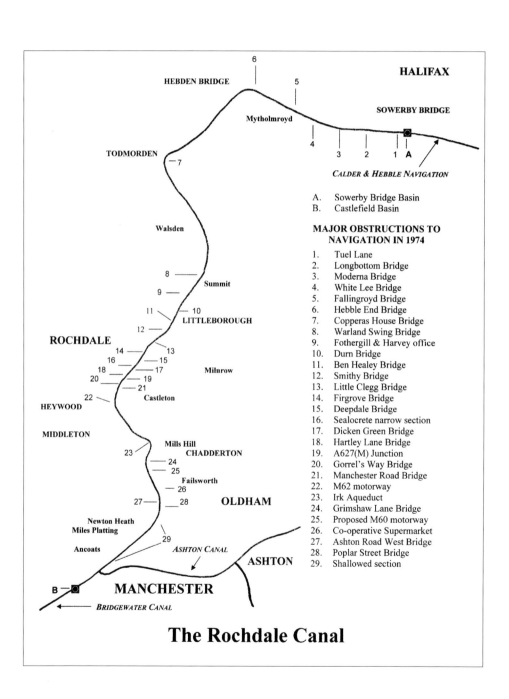

6
HEBDEN BRIDGE | 5
HALIFAX

Mytholmroyd
SOWERBY BRIDGE

4

TODMORDEN
—7
3 2 1 A

CALDER & HEBBLE NAVIGATION

A. Sowerby Bridge Basin
B. Castlefield Basin

Walsden

MAJOR OBSTRUCTIONS TO
NAVIGATION IN 1974

8
9
Summit

1. Tuel Lane
2. Longbottom Bridge
3. Moderna Bridge
4. White Lee Bridge
5. Fallingroyd Bridge
6. Hebble End Bridge
7. Copperas House Bridge
8. Warland Swing Bridge
9. Fothergill & Harvey office
10. Durn Bridge
11. Ben Healey Bridge
12. Smithy Bridge
13. Little Clegg Bridge
14. Firgrove Bridge
15. Deepdale Bridge
16. Sealocrete narrow section
17. Dicken Green Bridge
18. Hartley Lane Bridge
19. A627(M) Junction
20. Gorrel's Way Bridge
21. Manchester Road Bridge
22. M62 motorway
23. Irk Aqueduct
24. Grimshaw Lane Bridge
25. Proposed M60 motorway
26. Co-operative Supermarket
27. Ashton Road West Bridge
28. Poplar Street Bridge
29. Shallowed section

11
12
10
LITTLEBOROUGH

ROCHDALE
14
16
18
20
22
13
15
17
19
21
Milnrow

Castleton

HEYWOOD

MIDDLETON

Mills Hill
CHADDERTON
23
24
25
Failsworth
26
27
28
OLDHAM

Newton Heath
Miles Platting
29
Ancoats
ASHTON CANAL
ASHTON

B
MANCHESTER
BRIDGEWATER CANAL

The Rochdale Canal

INTRODUCTION

Two hundred years ago, three canals were built to provide major east–west transport arteries across the backbone of the Pennines in the north of England. To the north, the Leeds & Liverpool Canal followed the low-lying route through the Aire Gap but took a far too roundabout route to attract the important trade of Manchester. To the south, the Huddersfield Narrow Canal struck out on an almost direct line between the Ashton Canal linking to Manchester and the waterways of West Yorkshire, but it was to the same narrow gauge as the Ashton Canal. That required transhipment of goods to broader vessels in Huddersfield, or the use of small capacity short narrow boats able to travel on the narrow Huddersfield Canal and traverse the short locks of the broad Calder & Hebble Navigation. To gain a direct route it required an immensely long tunnel through the Pennines at Standedge that caused delays and congestion. Between these canals, the Rochdale Canal sought a course, not quite direct but not too tortuous, through the low level Ice Age meltwater channel between Littleborough and Todmorden. This avoided the necessity of a tunnel at the summit level, and the canal was built to the same broad gauge as the connecting Bridgewater Canal in the west and the Calder & Hebble Navigation in the east. It could hardly fail and, indeed, the Rochdale Canal proved to be the class act of the trans-Pennine canals.

The Rochdale Canal was built very quickly despite rising prices to pay for the Napoleonic Wars. It was open for trade from Rochdale to Yorkshire in 1798 and from end to end by 1804 – the pioneer of the trans-Pennine canals, years before the competing Leeds & Liverpool or Huddersfield Canals opened. Yet it was extremely well built and the canal carried a heavy trade throughout the nineteenth century. No doubt trade was affected by the development of competing railways, especially for longer distance traffic but the canal was able to trade successfully into the twentieth century. The development of motor transport rapidly brought about its demise, however, and by the outbreak of the Second World War there was no trade left on the canal, except for a few short movements in central Manchester.

Navigation on all but this short stretch in Manchester was formally abandoned in 1952 and the remaining Manchester length soon became almost impassable.

The lowering of road bridges, a supermarket built on the route of the canal, major motorway obstructions and general dereliction followed but not all was lost. Enthusiasts succeeded in seeing the central Manchester section open to navigation again by 1974, in a famous campaign to restore navigation to the Cheshire Ring of canals. Buoyed by that success, the Rochdale Canal Society was formed to promote restoration of the canal across the Pennines. The society was able to persuade local authorities to become involved in the campaign and won a major battle in a public inquiry into another proposed motorway blocking the canal that would effectively have put an end to ideas of restoration in Lancashire. The local authorities, especially Calderdale in West Yorkshire, became increasingly enthusiastic about the benefits that restoration of the canal could generate, bringing official recognition to the restoration campaign and a long search for funding that would eventually see the canal reopened to navigation from end to end in 2002.

As with all major waterway restoration projects carried out over a long period, the canal is far from perfect. No doubt much of the work needed to improve navigation will be carried out as essential maintenance but that may not be sufficient. Issues of water supply, in particular, need to be addressed. The bicentenary of the completion of the canal in 2004 could provide the impetus needed for consideration of how these improvements will be achieved.

For the sake of clarity, I refer in the text to the Manchester Outer Ring Road motorway that crosses the canal at Chadderton by its current title of the M60. Before the renumbering of the ring of motorways around Manchester and at the time of the public inquiry that forms the main subject of chapter seven, it was referred to as the M66.

The chapter headings are titles of songs recorded by, or films starring, the late Dame Gracie Fields, born in Rochdale in 1898, who became a huge star between the late 1920s and the 1950s, making fifteen films released between 1932 and 1946, featuring comedy songs and sentimental ballads. They do have a relevance to the themes of the chapters!

one

WE'RE GOING TO BE RICH

It is said that what Manchester thinks today, the rest of the world thinks tomorrow. That certainly was the case when the Duke of Bridgewater opened a canal from his coal mine at Worsley to Manchester in 1765. Overnight the price of coal in Manchester fell by half and profits from the canal and his mines made the Duke an immensely wealthy man. Soon there were plans for many other canals from promoters wishing to emulate the Duke's success, including the subject of this book, a remarkable proposal made the very next year to build a canal from Manchester to Rochdale, ten miles to the north east, that would then continue through the high moors of the Pennines from Lancashire into Yorkshire.

In mid-eighteenth century England most people still lived in the countryside but the population was growing, and especially the population of the towns. Agriculture was changing, with the enclosure of land bringing cheaper and more plentiful food. Manufacturing was expanding to supply new markets with goods. In the Pennine districts of Lancashire and Yorkshire, between Rochdale on the west flank of the hills and Halifax on the east, farmers had diversified into weaving woollen cloth. Over time, this had developed into an important, if still largely home-based, industry. The import of cotton was increasing too through the port of Liverpool, to satisfy the demands of the growing handloom-based cotton industry in south-east Lancashire, where Manchester was developing as the marketing and commercial centre of that trade. Transport was increasingly important to carry finished cloth to the markets and to the ports for export, and to bring in raw wool which the Pennine weavers were importing from further and further afield to meet the demand. However, the roads were bad. Wheeled traffic was frequently bogged-down in winter or wet weather and riders travelling any distance set out early to be ahead of the packhorse trains that clogged busy sections of road. Rochdale and Halifax were centres of a network of packhorse trails connecting hillside hamlets and were themselves joined by exposed routes across the high moorland, where in 1724 Daniel Defoe found that the Blackstonedge route had 'a frightful precipice on the one hand and uneven ground on the other'. Inadequate though they were, for a long time these had been the main cross-country transport routes, busy with lines of Galloway horses carrying cloth from local weavers and bringing lime and other goods into the area. Parliament had been granting the power to erect gates and toll bars to turnpike trustees in exchange for the trustees remaking and maintaining the highway since the beginning of the century, but progress was slow here in the arduous conditions of the high moors of the Pennines. Following an Act of Parliament in 1734, The Blackstonedge route improved but it was not until 1760 that Parliament approved a turnpike road along the easiest crossing of the South Pennines, through the low pass between the valleys of the eastward flowing river Calder and the westward flowing river Roch, and that route was not complete until 1781. Even with improved turnpike roads, served by a regular pattern of stagecoach services, highway travel was slow and only small loads could be carried; it was far better to carry bulk goods by water.

Rochdale and Halifax did not have the benefit of the water transport available to towns and villages on the coast or on rivers suitable for navigation. River and coastal craft could carry much larger loads with far less effort than the hard working packhorse, and by the early eighteenth century, rivers were improved to extend that benefit further inland. In Yorkshire, the river Aire was improved so that navigation was possible as far inland as Leeds and the river Calder was improved to Wakefield from its confluence with the Aire at Castleford. The first boats reached Wakefield in 1702. To the west of the Pennines, the rivers Mersey and Irwell were also made navigable and the first boats reached Manchester in 1734 and quays and warehouses were soon built there. To improve access to Halifax, John Smeaton was instructed in 1756 to survey the river Calder with the intention of making it navigable upstream of the Aire & Calder Navigation at Wakefield. An influential group from Rochdale, who also wished to benefit from improved transport to the east by navigation of the Calder and the turnpike road across Blackstonedge, joined in the subscribers to this, the Calder & Hebble Navigation. As a result, when an Act of Parliament was obtained, the navigation was planned to extend further up the Calder valley than originally intended, to Sowerby Bridge, a few miles south-west of Halifax. Work started almost immediately.

This extension of navigable water towards the Pennines from east and west was dependent on the making of rivers navigable but the engineering techniques were developing to be able to build entirely artificial waterways. A network of navigable canals could revolutionise transport. As we have seen, the man who was to launch the canal era was the Duke of Bridgewater. The Bridgewater Canal connecting the Duke's coal mine at Worsley to Manchester was not the first manmade cross-watershed canal in the British Isles but it was extremely influential. When it was open to Castlefield, Manchester, in 1765, the canal proved to be remarkably prof-itable for the Duke and immensely beneficial for Manchester. Promoters of other canals soon came forward, beginning with a scheme to connect Stoke-on-Trent to the river Trent by what we now know as the Trent & Mersey Canal approved by Parliament in 1766. The Duke of Bridgewater had employed James Brindley, a millwright, as the engineer for his canal and he was appointed as engineer for the Trent & Mersey. He became the foremost waterway engineer of these early years of the canal era, being involved with a whole series of canals that would create what he called a Grand Cross linking the rivers Trent, Mersey, Severn and Thames. At the same time Brindley was building a second arm of the Duke's Canal that would eventually connect to the Trent & Mersey at Preston Brook and then to the river Mersey at Runcorn and thus to Liverpool. The Mersey & Irwell Navigation and the Bridgewater Canal were built to suit the dimensions of Mersey Flats, the sailing barges of the Mersey Estuary, and the Aire & Calder and the Calder & Hebble Navigations to suit the dimensions of Humber Keels. These flats and keels were similar in size, fitting a lock of about 4.3m (14ft) in width, although keels were shorter, resulting in the relatively short locks of the Aire & Calder (as originally built) and the Calder & Hebble. When Brindley came to build the Trent & Mersey Canal, however, he chose to limit the costs of construction, especially of the long tunnel under Harecastle Hill, and to limit the amount of water needed to supply the locks of the canal by adopting a much narrower width. The Trent & Mersey and the other canals of Brindley's Grand Cross were built mainly as narrow canals, to a gauge allowing for boats about 2.1m (7ft) wide and 21m (70ft) long.

It was at this early stage in the development of the canal network that proposals were first put forward for what was to become the Rochdale Canal. Richard Townley, a local magistrate of Belfield Hall, Rochdale, called a meeting at The Union Flag Inn, Rochdale, in August 1766, to consider 'making surveys, plans and estimates of the intended canal from the Calder & Hebble Navigation [then still under construction] at Sowerby Bridge to the Bridgewater Canal at Manchester', which would 'join the east and west seas'. The forty-eight prominent local citizens present subscribed £237 4s 6d to enable a survey to begin.

No sooner had the plans been announced than pressure was brought to bear from nearby Bury, six miles to the west of Rochdale, for the canal to be taken to Manchester via Bury. This had some logic, but doubled the distance between Manchester and Rochdale. James Brindley, the acknowledged expert on these new canals, was appointed to carry out a survey. He was instructed to consider both routes. His estimates for a narrow canal like those he was building in the Midlands were submitted in October 1766. A direct route from Sowerby Bridge up the Calder Valley to Summit, where glacial meltwater from the Ice Age had cut the lowest crossing of the South Pennines, and then down the Roch Valley to Littleborough and Rochdale and the Irk Valley to Middleton and Manchester, would cost £79,180. The longer route, diverted to the north of Rochdale via Bury and then following the Irwell valley to Manchester, would cost £106,625.

Townley and his colleagues, including the Lord of the Manor, Lord Byron, and names such as Royds, Smith, Wood and Hamer that would be seen later as shareholders of the canal as eventually built, were unable to overcome the opposition of the faction pressing for the Bury route but they were unwilling to proceed with

The long-suffering packhorses, normally led in trains of around thirty horses, provided the only reliable transport across the Pennines for many years but they were hardly suitable for carrying bulky goods. (Keith Gibson)

the extra distance and cost. Then disastrous floods washed out much of the work still under construction on the river Calder between Wakefield and Sowerby Bridge so it was not until September 1770 that the whole twenty-four miles of the Calder & Hebble Navigation was open to Sowerby Bridge. The Rochdale project was abandoned or, at least, suspended for a quarter of a century.

It is convenient to think of the Lancashire textile industry as cotton-based and Yorkshire as wool-based, but the area between Rochdale and Halifax was the borderland between the two. The weaving of cotton spread to Rochdale and into the upper Calder Valley for sale in the Manchester market. Although there was a woollen cloth market in Rochdale, Halifax was the major market for woollen cloth in this part of the South Pennines, a dominance confirmed by the opening of the magnificent Piece Hall there in 1779. Fulling (the beating of woollen cloth with massive hammers to create a dense pile) had long been a factory-based operation, with a water-powered fulling mill at Hebden Bridge in the Calder Valley as early as 1429 but, from the late eighteenth century onwards, other processes beginning with the spinning of yarn and the carding and scribbling of wool were mechanised. As mechanical spinning was introduced in water-powered and soon steam-powered mills, cotton-spinning mills spread from Manchester to Rochdale and across the Pennines to the Calder Valley, where John Fielden built Clough Mill in Todmorden as early as 1786. By the end of the century, the Pennines accounted for almost one third of British wool textile production, with as much as two thirds of that production exported to Europe and North America.

Geography dictated that this trade in cotton and woollen cloth was mainly through the ports of Liverpool and Hull. As early as 1783, for instance, the Manchester market exported 250,000 cotton velveteens through the port of Hull. But clothiers even exported via Bristol, with around 150 packhorses leaving Manchester every week bound for the river Severn and onward carriage of the bales of cloth by water to that port. As the century progressed, the need for improved transport became greater. In 1875 the amateur Rochdale historian, William Robertson, noted that 'the transit of goods... by packhorses [was] remembered by some of the oldest inhabitants of Rochdale, and it [was] well-known that handloom weavers were often under the necessity of carrying their pieces to Manchester on their backs'.

Only a month before Townley's meeting at The Union Flag Inn, a similar meeting at The Sun Inn in Bradford decided to go ahead with plans for building a canal from the Aire & Calder Navigation at Leeds to Skipton and then, via the Aire Gap through the Pennines to the Lancashire Plain and Liverpool. The promoters of this, the Leeds & Liverpool Canal, just like the Rochdale party, saw the benefits of and the potential profits to be gained from a major west-east trade route. When it was eventually completed the Leeds & Liverpool Canal was 127 miles long, taking a very long way around to find the easiest crossing of the Pennines. By 1790, the Leeds & Liverpool Canal was open from Leeds to Gargrave on the Yorkshire side and from Liverpool to Wigan, but the canal was still incomplete across the Pennines.

The demand for improved bulk transport for the districts west of Sowerby Bridge was such that the proposal for a southern trans-Pennine canal was revived that same year when a meeting was called to consider extending the Calder & Hebble another five miles up the Calder Valley to Hebden Bridge. Rochdale people attended and suggested that the idea of a through canal to Manchester should be revived. A second meeting was called in Rochdale on 17 February 1791, which the later Canal Company's minute book noted was 'to take into consideration the desirable advantage likely to arise... by extending the two Navigable Canals from Manchester and Sowerby Bridge Wharfs, so as to make a Junct. thereof... '

Although the Duke of Bridgewater had found the money to build his canal from his own and borrowed resources, no individual or group of individuals had been able or willing to pay for the construction of the Trent & Mersey Canal. A joint stock company had been set up for that purpose, using money invested by shareholders in the company to pay the enormous cost of the canal. That set the pattern followed by most canals built at this time and would be by the proposed new canal – the Rochdale Canal. In April 1791, a committee was formed that would manage this company, if permission could be obtained to build the canal. George Travis, the Archdeacon of Chester, was appointed as chairman. Although he held the posts of Vicar of Eastham, curate of Bromborough and Rector of Handley, all places within a few miles of Chester, the Reverend Travis was from a

Archdeacon George Travis, the chairman of the committee proposing to build the Rochdale Canal and, later, the first chairman of the Company of Proprietors of the Rochdale Canal, as depicted on a memorial plaque in Chester Cathedral. (Robin Witter)

Rochdale family and, before studying in Cambridge, he had attended Manchester Grammar School. The new canal would follow approximately the line surveyed by Brindley. He had been dead for many years, however, and a new engineer would be required. The committee approached William Jessop, the leading engineer of this middle phase of the canal building era, but he had too many other commitments. Robert Whitworth, an almost equally experienced and qualified engineer, was similarly committed elsewhere. The committee turned to John Rennie. He would later gain recognition for engineering the Kennet & Avon and Lancaster Canals. William Crosley, a local surveyor from Brighouse, had already carried out a preliminary survey of the route. The committee appointed him to assist Rennie. Rennie was instructed to survey the route to produce a plan and estimates suitable for approval by Parliament, which, the committee decided in August, should include a branch into Oldham, and a long branch from Todmorden heading north-west through Cornholme, Holme Chapel and Worsthorne, skirting Burnley to join the route proposed for the Leeds & Liverpool Canal near Colne.

Brindley's plans had been for a narrow canal, but the Bridgewater, Mersey & Irwell, Calder & Hebble and the Leeds & Liverpool were all to a broad gauge. If the money could be found, the new canal should obviously be a broad canal. The committee was unable to make up its mind and William Crosley wrote to Rennie that he foresaw 'very florid debates' on this issue. Not only was this unresolved but the exact destination of the canal in Manchester was undecided too. The Duke of Bridgewater refused permission for a connection with his canal. The committee considered either building close to the Bridgewater so that transhipment over the intervening spur of land was possible, or connecting to the Mersey & Irwell Navigation, if the Navigation Company would agree.

Then issues became immensely more complex, with the return of the Bury party to the scene. Earlier in 1791, Parliament had approved the Manchester, Bolton & Bury Canal to connect Bolton & Bury to the Mersey & Irwell Navigation at Salford. A significant group of Manchester, Bolton & Bury share-holders proposed the Bury & Sladen Canal that would form an end-to-end junction with the Manchester Bolton & Bury at Bury and connect to the route of the Rochdale Canal at Sladen, near present day Littleborough. Beyond there, the Rochdale Canal proposal occupied the tight confines of the obvious route to Sowerby Bridge, so the Bury & Sladen promoters extended their project by proposing a new route through an immensely long tunnel under Blackstonedge and then to Sowerby Bridge and the Calder & Hebble Navigation via Ripponden and the Ryburn Valley. The Mersey & Irwell Navigation's support for this proposal led to the Duke of Bridgewater leaning more to the Rochdale proposal as the Bury route would deliver cross-Pennine traffic directly to the Mersey & Irwell, avoiding his canal's route to Runcorn and the Mersey but he still would not agree to actual terms for a connection. The Leeds & Liverpool Canal Company supported the Rochdale proposal because the link between Colne and Sowerby Bridge could provide extra trade and a more direct link between their canal and the western part of growing industrial West Yorkshire. They agreed to build the first part of the link from the junction at Colne to Worsthorne but that left the heavily locked section between there and Todmorden for the Rochdale company to construct.

A canal company could not forcibly take land that was not in its ownership, and the procedure for obtaining approval by Parliament was by this time well estab-lished. In effect, Parliament approved the route and gave the company powers to obtain the land needed, in exchange for the company allowing a public right of navigation on the canal. So a bill was submitted to Parliament with certain important issues remaining unresolved. The committee hoped that they had done all that was necessary to deflect the rival Bury & Sladen scheme, even though the promoters of that scheme had also submitted a bill for Parliamentary approval.

So focussed had the committee members been on the rivalry with the Bury scheme that they failed to appreciate the strength of objections to the proposals for the canal from the very people it was intended to serve: the millowners. They submitted a petition to Parliament against the new canal. There were:

> On the said rivers upwards of forty mills for the milling of woollen cloths, scrib-bling and spinning of wool and cotton and the grinding of corn which produce to the Proprietors upwards of £10,000 per annum. [Should] a diminution of water, sufficient to supply a canal, take place, the petitioners apprehend [the mills] may nearly be rendered useless in the summer months.

Faced by this opposition, the committee retained Robert Mylne, an expert on water supply issues, to represent them before the Parliamentary committee that was considering the bill. He was to explain how Rennie's proposals for steam-powered pumps to bring water to the canal should ensure that the millowners would not be inconvenienced.

Parliament was unconvinced and the Bill was lost. Rennie was so moved as to write a verse in his notebook:'On a fair and virtuous young maiden call'd the Rochdale Canal who was barbarously murder'd near Old Palace Yard, Westminster on the night of 21 March 1792'. The Bury & Sladen Canal also failed to gain Parliamentary approval, and the Bury party suggested that the Rochdale people should join them to seek approval for at least the Bury to Sladen section of their proposal. This idea was dismissed by the Rochdale Committee – now strengthened by the addition of Dr Drake, the Vicar of Rochdale, and John Gilbert junior – who decided that they would proceed in a similar manner by putting to Parliament a plan for the Lancashire side of the canal from Manchester to Littleborough only. They soon realised that this would leave the door open for the Bury party to propose a route to Sowerby Bridge. The only sensible course was to continue with plans to build the entire canal. The Bury party announced their intention to resubmit a Bill to Parliament for their canal through to Sowerby Bridge. That at last persuaded the Duke of Bridgewater to agree terms for a connection with the Rochdale, and to offer his support in Parliament.

To placate the millowners, Crosley was instructed to survey for water supply reservoirs so that at least the rivers Roch, Irk and Medlock on the Lancashire side would not have water taken directly from them to supply the canal and Rennie proposed a series of reservoirs on the high moors of the Pennines to feed the canal. This reduced the opposition from millowners, indeed those in the Todmorden area (whose need for the canal was perhaps the greatest because of their remote location) supported the plan, but many in the Calder Valley still saw no change in the likely effect on their water supply.

So a second Bill was submitted to Parliament. This time the committee was quite clear that it intended to build a narrow canal. The more that was expended on seeking permission for the canal, the less enthusiasm there was for a broad canal. Even for a narrow canal, Rennie now estimated the cost, with reservoirs, at £291,929. The branch from Todmorden to Colne was no longer proposed. It would be costly to construct, and the support of the Leeds & Liverpool Canal seemed less important than overcoming local objections. Also, the plan to build a branch into Oldham was discontinued. By this time, work had started on building the Ashton Canal, approved by Parliament as a narrow canal leading from the likely route of the Rochdale at Piccadilly, Manchester to Ashton-under-Lyne. It would include a branch northwards to Hollinwood, just to the south of Oldham, that was likely to take the trade that might have been attracted to the Rochdale.

Despite all their efforts, the committee had still not done enough to persuade Parliament that the fears of the millowners were unjustified and the arguments for or against the Rochdale or the Bury & Sladen plans before the Parliamentary committee considering the proposals could have done little to give Parliament sufficient faith to approve the plan. The Bill was again lost but this time by only one vote; and so was the Bury & Sladen plan, by a rather larger margin.

For a third time the promoters began to prepare for another Bill in Parliament, trying even harder than before to reach an understanding with the millowners and seeking petitions in favour from as far away as Hull, Bristol, Gloucester, Tewkesbury and the Potteries.

To complicate matters even further, what Parliament might see as a third alternative to the Rochdale or the Bury & Sladen routes, was now proposed as an extension of the Ashton Canal directly through the Pennines via a tunnel not quite as long as that required for the Bury scheme under Blackstonedge but still over three miles long, at Standedge. From there the Huddersfield Canal would follow the Colne Valley to Huddersfield where it would connect to Sir John Ramsden's Canal, the short branch canal from the Calder & Hebble at Cooper Bridge to Huddersfield. Like the Rochdale proposals, this canal would be a narrow canal; indeed to build it otherwise would be pointless, as construction of the Ashton Canal was already well underway to the narrow gauge.

Possibly, partly in desperation, but probably mainly because John Rennie was much occupied with the Kennet & Avon Canal, the Rochdale Committee again approached William Jessop. It must have seemed a slim hope that Jessop would be able to help them. The large profits made by the early canals were attracting so many speculators to join local promoters of canal schemes and Parliament was considering so many plans, that there was talk of there being a 'canal mania'. Jessop's services were much in demand. He was the leading engineer of the time. He had learned his trade as an apprentice to Smeaton while the Calder & Hebble was under construction and

William Jessop, the foremost engineer of the middle years of the canal building era, and engineer to the Rochdale Canal; sketched by his friend, the architect and artist, George Dance, in 1796. (National Portrait Gallery, London)

19

had worked on many canal projects. His main commissions at this time were as engineer for the Ellesmere Canal (we now know that as the Llangollen), the Barnsley Canal, and the Grand Junction Canal (now the Grand Union). The Grand Junction was the most important project of this period, by-passing the southern Oxford Canal and the river Thames to provide a direct route from the south Midlands to London and when they had appointed him, the committee of the Grand Junction company had considered him to be 'the first engineer of the kingdom'.

Perhaps Jessop thought that had he helped the Rochdale Committee earlier they might not have been in this predicament. Perhaps he believed the issues had already been thoroughly gone over by Rennie. We will never know the reason, but no doubt to the committee's immense relief, Jessop decided that 'though much engaged' he would do what he could to help. And what he did was significant and prompt. His report to the committee of February 1794 was considered so important that the *Manchester Mercury* printed it in full. Jessop's opinion that the canal could be provided with a water supply from reservoirs 'without taking any water from the mills which could be useful to them' was crucial, and he suggested the sites of two large reservoirs at Hollingworth and Blackstonedge.

Parliament yet again considered the alternative proposals for a canal across the South Pennines: the Rochdale plan, the Bury & Sladen plan and the additional plan for the Huddersfield Canal. With the support of Jessop before the Parliamentary committee, petitions of support from all over the country, and less opposition from the millowners whose fears now seemed to have been overcome, the Rochdale Canal Act was at last approved on 4 April 1794. The Huddersfield Canal was approved on the same day but the directly competitive Bury & Sladen plan failed yet again.

No doubt the committee breathed an immense sigh of relief and celebratory drinks were drunk in Rochdale and Manchester. There was a catch in the small print of Parliament's approval, however. The Rochdale committee had come down firmly in favour of a narrow canal that, together with the Ashton and the Huddersfield, would have created a group of northern narrow canals of the same gauge as the main Midlands network, but Parliament required the canal to be a broad canal. That would avoid the need to tranship goods from broad-beam craft to narrow boats at Manchester or Sowerby Bridge. It was certainly sensible as a theory of sound planning but the share capital authorised by Parliament in the new Canal Company remained based on Rennie's estimate of costs for a narrow canal, with the power to raise an extra £100,000 if needed. A broad canal would cost considerably more than a narrow canal. This was a matter that would have to be dealt with; but that could wait. The committee formed themselves into the Company of Proprietors of the Rochdale Canal, with George Travis still as chairman. William Crosley staked out the line on the ground ready for Jessup to plan the detail of the canal.

It may seem strange after all the work that had gone into obtaining approval for the canal that there were no detailed plans and that the costs presented to

Parliament were those produced by Rennie based solely on his experience and educated guesswork. As with all major schemes then (and even now), the promoters could not afford to sanction the expensive hours of detailed design work until approval was obtained. The committee had already spent £12,000 obtaining permission to proceed with the canal. Investors would not have been willing to speculate on design fees that would have gone to waste if permission was not forthcoming. Despite his heavy workload on other schemes, Jessop stayed on as engineer for the company. The canal would be built to his design, although largely to the route previously chosen by Rennie and Crosley.

The building of the canal was, as with most large projects, under the control of a resident engineer. It was his responsibility to see that the details were correctly set out on the ground, to control contractors working on the canal and to ensure that work was to a good standard and carried out within an agreed time. The Rochdale Company and Jessop were much better served by their choice of resident engineers than many canal companies were. Most canal companies, at this time when so many canals were under construction, had no choice than to take whoever they could get to control the work, but the Rochdale Company already knew the abilities of William Crosley and he was appointed resident engineer.

Jessop submitted a report to the 17 June 1794 committee meeting with detailed proposals for building the canal. He spelled out his intention to minimise waste of water by making all the locks, insofar as that was possible, with a 3m (10ft) rise, except in Manchester. Here the locks on the probably heavily used length between the junctions with the Bridgewater Canal at Castlefield basin and the Ashton Canal would each have a rise of about 2.1m (7ft) to reduce the time taken in locking through. The most significant change to Rennie's proposals was the abandonment of a summit tunnel. Jessop had successfully built Butterley Tunnel on the Cromford Canal with Benjamin Outram as his assistant. Outram was now engaged on the rival Huddersfield Canal, which included the longest tunnel built on the British canal system at Standedge. Jessop may already have had hints of the difficulties that he was to face with the tunnels at Braunston and Blisworth on the Grand Junction Canal and he took the view that unknown conditions underground were best left unknown if any practical alternative was available. Instead of Rennie's 3,000m long tunnel, Jessop built a deep cutting at Summit with an extra seven locks on each side to reach that higher level.

Jessop supplied details for the building of locks, bridges and culverts, for the building of the reservoirs at Hollingworth and Blackstonedge and for the method of digging the deep summit cutting. He suggested work should start early on the embankment needed at Slack's Valley between Chadderton and Failsworth, to allow time for consolidation.

Work began at Sowerby Bridge, on the summit cutting and between the Ashton Canal junction and Castlefield, and very soon contractors could be found on most of the route between Rochdale and Sowerby Bridge. When Jessop inspected the works in January 1796, he was able to report to the committee that: 'the works of masonry are in general sound and substantial and that upon the whole there appears to have been good management in the conduct of the work and economy in expenditure'. How lucky the Rochdale Company had been in having William Crosley to control the work. The Huddersfield Canal to the south was already in trouble with an inexperienced resident engineer and a committee lacking the ability to plan the work. Late in 1796 Crosley died but again the sun shone on the Rochdale Company. They were able to appoint Thomas Bradley, the Calder & Hebble Navigation's experienced engineer. He stayed as resident engineer, helped by Thomas Townshend, until 1801, when he returned to the Calder & Hebble. Townshend successfully continued alone until he left in 1802 to be replaced by Crosley's son, William Crosley junior.

Progress was such that the canal was opened between Sowerby Bridge and Todmorden on 24 April 1798, and then through to Rochdale on 21 December that year. The committee yacht *Travis* and the Calder & Hebble Navigation's *Savile* were the first boats to arrive with canon fire, flags and a crowd of thousands to watch.

The feeder channels and reservoirs at Hollingworth and Blackstonedge were sufficiently finished to be able to supply the canal from Rochdale to the east but work on the section in Manchester stopped until water could be supplied from Rochdale.

Trade started immediately, with the Canal Company encouraging long distance trade. Edward Thompson and John Handley from Hull were persuaded to provide an inclusive price for carriage by boat from Hull to Rochdale, and by road from there to Manchester. This must have proved unsatisfactory because the company were offering a similar service themselves by January 1801. The company co-operated with the Calder & Hebble Navigation to offer a service between Manchester and Leeds, and Aire & Calder boats worked onto the canal.

Trade was rising but it might have been harder to come by than had been hoped because the canal had been built and was being operated at a time of war with Revolutionary and Napoleonic with France. Not only were taxes raised dramatically to pay for the war but the local textile industry, suffering from severe disruption on occasions because of blockades of ports by both sides preventing the export of cloth, was terribly depressed. Prices rose dramatically with the cost of household commodities almost double in 1801 what they had been when building work started on the canal. Like all canals built at this time, the original estimate of the cost was inevitably insufficient. With prices rising at that rate, every ton of sand and every ton of lime for mortar, for instance, would cost twice what had been expected. Matters were particularly bad on the Rochdale Canal because the original estimate was for a narrow canal, yet Parliament had committed the company to build a broad one, with larger locks, wider bridges and a broader channel than originally planned. The rate of progress of building up the Calder Valley and over the difficult central Pennine section with its deep summit cutting had been extraordinary but work slowed dramatically on cutting the canal to Manchester after the canal was open to Rochdale. It was not until

October 1802 that the next section of canal was opened to Castleton by 'the yacht *Travis* attended by crowds of neighbouring people' as *The Manchester Mercury* reported.

Parliament had been approached again in 1800 when a second Act of Parliament granted the company the power to borrow an extra £100,000. The Act also allowed the company to increase its tolls and authorised slight changes from Rennie's route on the final section to Manchester. Work must have almost halted for a time here. The situation was not as bad as on the Huddersfield Canal to the south. Many shareholders in that canal were reluctant to honour calls on their shares (the procedure being that only a part of the value of a share had to be put down initially, with the remainder provided when called upon by the company), although a few recalcitrant Rochdale shareholders were also pursued in 1802. In 1804, a third Act of Parliament authorised the company to raise another £70,000 in a complex way, by converting the nominal value of the existing 2,861 £120 shares to £60 and then issuing a similar number of new £60 shares that were sold to existing shareholders for £20 and to new subscribers for between £50 and £64.

The speed of construction over the Pennine summit to Rochdale at a time of economic difficulty must have astounded the shareholders of the Leeds & Liverpool Canal, which would not be complete until 1816, and the Huddersfield Canal where the company was struggling to finance its immense tunnel and which did not open until 1811. Whatever breathing space those shareholders might have felt they had gained as work on the final section of the Rochdale slowed was only to be short lived. The canal was complete by the end of 1804. The *Morning Chronicle* told how the canal:

> was opened [on 21 December] in great style. The bells at Manchester commenced ringing at half past two, and the companies' passage boat and yacht, the *Savile* and *Travis* were greeted from the banks for a great distance by an immense concourse of spectators, with many a vociferous cheer of approbation. [The] two vessels were filled with the gentlemen proprietors and their friends attended by the band of the Fourth Class Volunteer who continued to play many loyal and patriotic tunes. Each gentleman, together with every servant and workman of the company wore in his hat a blue ribbon, with the inscription of gold letters 'Success to the Rochdale Canal', and on the flag of the yacht was inscribed 'Royal Rochdale Canal'.

As we are used to the spin of publicists and advertisers, we might be sceptical that the company's annual report for 1805 said:

> considering the magnitude of the works and the difficulties of the undertaking, few canals have been prosecuted with more uninterrupted success. The masonry and other parts of the work have hitherto stood the test, with fewer misfortunes than are commonly experienced in such undertakings. And what adds to the merit is that few tracts of country have been so unfavourable as the greatest part of the line.

The Rochdale Canal crosses the Pennines via the Ice Age meltwater channel between Littleborough and Todmorden. Here is the summit pound looking east, with Longlees Lock (No.36), the first on the descent into the Calder Valley. (David Evans)

Our scepticism would be totally unfounded. The canal was very well built with superb stonework. Without doubt, the Rochdale was the class act of the trans-Pennine waterways. In his *Lives of the Engineers* (1862), Samuel Smiles commented that 'whoever examines the works… will admit that the mark of a master's hand is unmistakably stamped upon them'. Although he seemed unaware that Jessop had replaced Rennie as the canal's engineer, the sentiment remains accurate.

The canal was 32 miles long with 92 locks. From its junction with the Calder & Hebble Navigation at Sowerby Bridge, it climbed by 36 locks up the Calder Valley through Luddenden Foot, Mytholmroyd, Hebden Bridge and Todmorden to the summit pound 180m (600ft) above sea level. It then fell quickly by 12 locks to Littleborough, confined in the tight contours of the Roch Valley until the valley widened where the canal turned south out of the valley between Rochdale and Milnrow. From there the canal left the high ground behind as it continued a more gentle descent through a further 44 locks, crossing the river Irk on an aqueduct to the north of Chadderton and the tributary Slacks Valley by an embankment, before turning south-eastwards again at Failsworth. The climb down to Manchester followed a route almost midway between the rivers Irk and Medlock through Miles Platting, Newton Heath and Ancoats, to join the Bridgewater Canal at Castlefield. Although I have listed some of the places alongside the canal, apart from Manchester, they were then mainly very small villages or mere collections of dwellings, very different to the modern settlements. For much of the way the scenery was (and still is in parts) magnificent and the canal simply went about its business in a quiet businesslike way. Waterways writer Anthony Burton put his finger on what made the Rochdale Canal such an extraordinary feat of high quality engineering in his book *The Great Days of the Canals* (1989). He said that its 'most remarkable feature is, paradoxically, that it has no remarkable features – no great tunnels, nor even extravagant aqueducts on a canal that crosses the Pennines at their wildest'.

The reservoirs that would supply water to the canal were not all complete by the opening day, indeed work continued until 1827 before the final arrangement of reservoirs was in use. The major system of seven high level reservoirs was grouped on Blackstonedge: Gadding, Warland, Light Hazzels, White Holme and Blackstonedge Reservoirs on the high moorland with Upper Chelburn and Lower Chelburn on lower slopes nearer the canal, all feeding by a complex arrangement of feeder channels to the west end of the summit pound. The largest reservoir, Hollingworth, on the hillside between Littleborough and Milnrow, was so large that it was known as a Hollingworth Lake – no nonsense about a reservoir for an expanse of water of this scale. Had Rennie's tunnel been built, Hollingworth Lake

I have found no drawings of the early boats on the canal. Daisy, seen here at Derdale, Todmorden in the early years of the twentieth century, was typical of the late nineteenth-century broad-beam horse-drawn boats. (Courtesy of David Evans)

would have fed the canal by gravity but with a higher summit level, a steam pump was necessary to take water to a long feeder that included a tunnel on its way to the summit pound. In 1857, a new supply channel was cut, taking Hollingworth Lake water to the canal below Littleborough and the pump was abandoned.

With the canal complete and the income from tolls paid by carriers increasing, the company set about putting its finances in the best order possible by paying off the debts incurred in building the canal. A fourth Act of Parliament allowed the company to make a further call of £25 per share issued, so that the 5,722 shares issued had a nominal value of £85 each. Most shareholders must have thought the extra investment worthwhile because the company bought in and cancelled only 59 shares. Whether they were wise to invest further would depend on the success of the canal in attracting trade. Before we turn to that, you may be wondering how much the canal had cost, compared to Rennie's original estimate of £291,929. I am unlikely to be more successful than waterways historian Charles Hadfield was in unravelling the complex financial arrangements approved by Parliament, the loans taken out by the company and the interest paid on those loans, and the amount of toll income that the company was able to spend on completing the building of the canal. In *The Canals of North West England, Volume 2*, written jointly with Gordon Biddle (1970), he estimated that the cost was 'rather over £600,000'. Bearing in mind that the canal was a broad canal rather than the narrow canal Rennie costed and that it was well built and built quickly, at a time of dramatically rising prices, one can only conclude that Jessop, the company and their resident engineers had done remarkably well.

two

SING AS WE GO

With the canal open from end to end, trade increased. There was new traffic using the Rochdale Canal as a route from east to west, and local traffic on the Lancashire side between Rochdale and Manchester and beyond. The Canal Company did everything within its powers to increase this traffic, instructing its wharfinger at Manchester that he must 'use his exertions in laying himself out and soliciting goods in Manchester'. Care was taken to ensure that the energetic efforts of the Huddersfield Canal Company to attract traffic to their still unfinished canal did not succeed. Agents working for the company were told that if they were found receiving 'emolument from any other concern' they would be 'discharged as soon as their accounts [were] made up'.

Water supply, or the lack of it, was an issue of concern for the company and probably also for the boatmen in the early days. Work continued on the reservoir system, with Light Hazzles and White Holme reservoirs not yet complete. The company employed additional lock keepers 'to aid and assist in passing the locks, in order to their greater safety and expedition, and for preservation of water'. A programme of building lock keepers' cottages began.

Because of the economic depression resulting from the Napoleonic Wars, trade did not at first develop as quickly as the company had hoped. In 1807, the committee decided to enter into the canal carrying business themselves by building three boats to provide a regular return service between Manchester and Rochdale. Agents were appointed to represent the company further afield in seeking trade from the port in Liverpool and from the river Trent in Gainsborough. However, trade was increasing. In 1808 Thomas Carver of Halifax started operation from Dale Street in Manchester, and – perhaps more important – Pickfords started an express service from an arm off the canal at nearby Lower Dickenson Street where they provided a warehouse, a dry-dock and a boatbuilding yard. They operated a fleet of narrow boats from here and from a base in London to provide a frequent service operating to a timetable. Known as flyboats, these craft worked fast with regular changes of crew and horses through the day and night. Lock balance beams were painted white to help the crews maintain a schedule that required them to deliver goods from Manchester to Littleborough in nine hours and to Todmorden in twelve hours.

Locally based craft using the canal were built to the maximum dimensions possible to fit within the locks, so that a Rochdale Canal Flat was 21.9m (72ft) long and 4.3m (14ft 2ins) wide, although many craft working on the canal had different dimensions. The West Country Keels of the Calder & Hebble Navigation were shorter at 17.3m (57ft) to fit within the locks of that waterway; indeed a Rochdale-length boat could not pass beyond Sowerby Bridge. Unless a short boat was used throughout, there was always some transhipment of goods between vessels there. In addition to the Pickford's flyboats, other narrow boats traded from the Ashton Canal or even the Midlands' narrow canal network. Eventually other craft would be found; broad craft from the Manchester Bolton & Bury Canal or from the Leeds & Liverpool Canal, when that canal was connected to the Bridgewater Canal by the Leigh Branch and even the occasional small coasting craft travelling across country, perhaps on the way to the Isle of Man or Ireland, with its mast lowered for the trip. Because of the shorter length of Calder & Hebble craft, the locks between Rochdale and Sowerby Bridge had been built with a second set of recesses for lock gates in the stonework at the Calder & Hebble length. Using these, the volume of water needed to fill a lock would be reduced and precious water saved. Puzzlingly, the extra gates were apparently never fitted.

In an engineering work of genius, Jessop designed the canal through the tight confines and steep gradients of the Pennine valleys so that, apart from locks and bridges, the only significant engineering features were two modest aqueducts over the rivers Irk and Calder. This is the Calder Aqueduct at Hebden Bridge. (David Evans)

To better control the growth of trade and the carrying out of the company's business, John Crossley was appointed as superintendent in 1810 at a salary of £300 a year, which rose to £500 a year in 1817. He was a member of the managing committee of the company; in modern terms we would expect him to have been designated the managing director or the chief executive officer. He must have been satisfied at the progress being made to increase trade as in 1811 the company withdrew from the carrying business itself and sold the Rochdale – Manchester boats to a carrier, Job Cogswell, who continued the service.

That same year the Huddersfield Canal finally opened. Although trade must have been affected to some extent, there was no noticeable drop in carrying on the Rochdale Canal. The Huddersfield Canal never had a chance of offering real competition to the Rochdale, despite being a shorter route. It was limited to narrow boat dimensions: loads had to be transhipped to Calder & Hebble sized broad-beam boats at Huddersfield or carried in special short, narrow boats able to fit the short locks of the Calder & Hebble and the narrow locks of the Huddersfield. The immense tunnel at Standedge made the boatmen's passage difficult and they were often delayed by congestion in the tunnel. To make matters even worse, the Huddersfield Company struggled to offer toll rates that were competitive with the Rochdale Canal because tolls also had to be paid to the separately owned Sir John Ramsden's Canal and Ashton Canal.

Coal became the major commodity carried on the canal, with a doubling of the tonnage carried from 42,509 tons in 1812 to 95,470 tons in 1819. This huge increase in just seven years mirrored a rapid building of new steam-powered textile mills. Coal mined in Lancashire was carried to the west of the canal and Yorkshire-mined coal to the east, Littleborough being the place where coal from neither east nor west had a clear cost advantage. In this same period, other cargoes increased to feed the building boom: stone from 26,033 tons to 42,255 tons, timber from 3,186 tons to 6,270 tons and lime from 11,735 tons to 13,458 tons. Lime was important; not just for use as a fertiliser but as a main ingredient of the soft building mortars and plasters of the time, before the adoption of cement in the frequently too hard mortars used today. The amount of corn increased from 20,375 tons to 40,553 tons to feed the growing population attracted to work in the new mills. However, the most intriguing figures in the statistics of trade at this time are for what were described as 'merchandise' and 'sundries.' It is intriguing because we do not really know what merchandise and sundries included. Merchandise saw a huge increase from 5,793 tons to 21,122 tons, but sundries, the largest category in 1812 and second only to coal in 1819, had a much smaller growth from 82,795 tons to 87,650 tons. Groceries and similar items seem unlikely to account for these high figures. I suspect that they included finished cloth carried from the immediate locality and the cotton mills of Manchester for export via Hull. Raw wool was represented by a separate category that grew from 3,070 tons in 1812 to 4,452 tons in 1819; not quite as large an increase as we might expect with the rapid rise in the number of mills, but most of the new mills along the

The terminal basin of the Calder & Hebble Navigation, Sowerby Bridge, with a boat being loaded or unloaded on the Rochdale Canal in the background. (Courtesy of Rochdale Canal Society).

route of the canal were cotton mills. No figures are available for the bales of raw cotton, the tonnage of which must have increased – presumably this is somewhere in the merchandise or sundries categories. It might be interesting to research these figures further but for our purposes, the important figures are the totals. The tonnage carried on the canal increased from 199,623 tons in 1812 to 317,050 tons in 1819.

The Canal Company became profitable, with a first dividend of £1 per share being paid in 1811. Dividends paid in subsequent years varied between 13s 4d and £2 6s 8d until 1821 when the dividend increased to £4; a figure then paid every year until 1835. Perhaps the shareholders would be rich after all. The committee was still spending on improving the water supply with Light Hazzles and White Holme reservoirs being brought into use, and on building warehouses to encourage trade. The company had its main wharves and warehouses at Piccadilly (Manchester), Rochdale and Sowerby Bridge, and others at Todmorden and Gauxholme. Trade was also encouraged in other ways. The company helped Job Cogswell, the carrier who had taken over the Rochdale – Manchester service, and the Rochdale and Halifax Merchants Company to operate to Wakefield by paying all or part of the cost of agents for the carriers there and other carriers were helped by loans to buy boats. The future looked so bright that the directors decided in November 1822 that 'a Gateway built of stone rusticated, [would] be erected at the entrance into the Manchester Wharf, between the new office and the Warehouse'.

However, there was a potential cloud drifting over the horizon: the smoke from the steam engines of the railway. Speculation in canal shares had been a way of getting rich quick at the time the canal was built but the mania for canal shares was nothing compared to the clamour for shares in railway companies that would develop after George Stephenson built the Stockton to Darlington Railway and the Liverpool to Manchester Railway. When the company began to receive letters from shareholders worried about the proposed Liverpool & Manchester Railway, the committee instructed the treasurer to reply that 'the committee do not view the measure with much alarm'. If that really was the company members' view, they were not alone in their misconception: the Duke of Wellington thought it unlikely that 'these machines will ever force themselves into general use'. But it may have been a political response because three months later, at its meeting on 24 April 1823, the committee instructed that the company's financial affairs should be conducted entirely in secret so as to limit the information available to any potentially competing railway that may be proposed.

At this time, six canal carrying companies had space permanently allocated to them in the company's Manchester warehouses: The Rochdale & Halifax Merchants' Company; The Manchester & Liverpool Union Company; John Thompson & Company; Barnaby, Faulkner, Reeder & Company; James Veevers; and George Thornton. Many carriers on the canal were based at Castlefield Basin including: J.G. Amos & Co.; Antwis & Sturland; Samuel Bache; Thomas Bache; Richard Barrows; Thomas Best; Coffield & Co.; Crockett Salkeld & Co.; Crowley Hicklin & Co.; Danks & Tyler; Edward & James Green; Mathew Heath; William Henshall; J. Kenworthy & Son; Kenworthy & Holt; Leeds Union Co.; Manchester Grocers' Co.; John Morris & Co.; Charles Moseley; The Marquis of Stafford; Moss, Henshall & Co.; John Simpson; Snell Robins & Co.; Soresby & Flack; James Suton; The Shardlow Boat Co.; John Whitehouse & Sons; and Worthington & Co. Then from Dale Street were operating: David Bellhouse & Sons; Barnby Faulkner; The Manchester & Liverpool Union Co.; John Palmer; Reeder & Co.; Rochdale & Halifax Merchants' Co.; Thomas Smith; John Thompson & Co.; George Thornton; James Veevers & Co.; Wakefield Traders; and William Wakeman. This list does not claim to be a comprehensive list of carriers on the canal. There were others operating from their own wharves such as Pickford's, or based at other locations on the canal such as Rochdale or Sowerby Bridge and many carriers traded onto the canal from neighbouring waterways. For a time, there was a passenger service between Rochdale and Manchester. Maybe the boats – known as packet boats after short sea ferries – were crowded but imagine the comfort of a smooth water-borne trip compared to the jolting and bruising ride of a stagecoach. It only took seven hours between Rochdale and Manchester. Surprisingly, passenger packet boats were only popular in England in the North West with similar services to Manchester on the Bridgewater, Ashton and Manchester, Bolton & Bury Canals. Passengers even travelled over the full length of the canal on occasions. The *Halifax Guardian* on 22 June 1839 reported that

Tiger, a Calder & Hebble size keel, had been chartered to take German emigrant 'agriculturalists and mechanics' between the ports of Hull and Liverpool to a new life in the USA. A more luxurious passenger boat also appeared on the canal in the form of the committee's new inspection yacht, The *Rochdale*, built by Smith & Murrow in Liverpool for the princely sum of £320 in 1832.

In that same year, the Canal Company was offered land to build a branch canal from the main line of the canal at Maden Fold, south of Castleton 1½ miles west to Heywood. As the land was available, there was no need for Parliamentary powers to build this extension; although as a result navigation on the branch would be at the company's discretion with no public rights. Being assured that traffic would justify the expense, an extraordinary meeting of shareholders on 3 August 1833 authorised the purchase of the land and the construction of the branch. Work started immediately and the new Heywood branch was officially opened by a trip on the line by *The Rochdale* on 10 April 1834. The company provided a warehouse for traders in Heywood.

The Liverpool & Manchester Railway opened in 1829 and brought even more trade to the Rochdale route. The total tonnage carried increased in the ten years between the opening of that railway and 1839 to 875,436 tons, and tolls received from carriers in the same period grew from £38,417 to £62,712. The company increased the dividend paid per share to £6, but the shadow of railway competition was growing darker month by month especially when a potentially competing railway reached Littleborough from Manchester in 1839. With it came an end to the passenger packet boat service on the main line of the canal, although a connecting service ran from the Heywood branch to meet trains at the station at Castleton for a short time.

The new railway, the Manchester & Leeds, must have been occupying the minds of the members of the committee of the Canal Company since at least 1830, when a Bill had first been introduced to Parliament seeking authority to build this railway across the Pennines. The route had been surveyed by George Stephenson who was assisted by Thomas Gooch, whose brother Daniel would become the locomotive engineer and, ultimately, chairman of the Great Western Railway. The Canal Company succeeded in delaying consideration of the railway Bill. It was lost when Parliament was dissolved. A second bill reached the committee stage and also failed, but, like the Canal Company's promoters before them, the railway promoters did not give in easily. A third Bill was submitted to Parliament, with Stephenson again as engineer and surveyor. The main central Pennine section of the route would be closely parallel to the canal through Littleborough and down the Calder Valley to Sowerby Bridge, although there would be a long tunnel at Summit. From Sowerby Bridge, the railway would continue down the Calder Valley to Wakefield. From there it would reach Leeds via a connection with the proposed North Midland Railway at Normanton. The Company of Proprietors of the Rochdale Canal naturally objected, saying that:

the great public advantage offered by the Rochdale Canal, the serious investment upon that undertaking and the small return... yielded to the company give them the most genuine hope that Parliament will, by rejecting the Railway Bill, leave them in undisturbed possession of their property.

With the success of the nearby Liverpool & Manchester Railway, Parliament was not moved by the company's hopes and the railway was approved on 4 July 1836. Work began the following year, after a second Act of Parliament authorised minor changes to the route and, as we have seen, Littleborough was reached by 1839. The tunnel at Summit proved difficult to build and there was considerable loss of life; perhaps justifying Jessop's concern about a tunnel on the canal. It was not until March 1841 that the railway was opened throughout. Two ceremonial trains each pulled by two engines – *Stephenson & Kenyon* and *Stanley & Lancaster* – traversed the route from Manchester to Leeds. On the next day when public services started, as many as 3,100 passengers were carried from Littleborough to Manchester.

Canal companies throughout the country were falling into railway ownership, often before the competing railway was built. The Ashton Canal went to the Sheffield, Ashton-under-Lyne and Manchester Railway, and the Huddersfield Canal would fall in 1844 to what soon became the London & North Western Railway. To the canal shareholders it made sense to seek the safety of the guaranteed return on their investment that the railways offered and it was logical for the railways to buy out the competition, especially when the canal might bring in supplies vital to the construction of the new railway. However, the Rochdale Canal, for a time, remained proudly independent.

The railways were proving to be brilliant at creating a brand new trade – the mass movement of passengers – and, despite early attempts by the Manchester & Leeds Railway to persuade carriers to transfer their trade to the railway, they were not immediately anxious to take over the bulk haulage of products, especially coal. Slow-moving heavy freight trains could clog up their lines to the detriment of passenger traffic. There was, however, an immediate loss of some trade from the canal, with the tonnage carried falling to 667,311 tons in 1842. Tolls were cut dramatically to tempt trade back to the canal; that brought the tonnage up to a high of 979,443 tons in 1845. But the extra trade gained had a price. Tolls paid by carriers to use the canal had been reduced to such an extent that total receipts were only £28,695 that year, compared to the £62,712 of 1839. Nevertheless, even at that reduced income level, the Rochdale Canal remained sufficiently profitable to pay a dividend of £3 per share, although shareholders must have been concerned that each share they held with a nominal value of £85 had actually been worth £150 had they wished to sell it in 1841, but would only sell for £40 in 1843. Pressure from carriers who played off the canal against the railway succeeded in bringing the rates down on both and as early as September 1841, Captain Laws of the Manchester & Leeds Railway Company suggested that the companies should agree a fair rate. Negotiations continued for some time between the Company of Proprietors of the Rochdale Canal, the Calder & Hebble Navigation, the Aire & Calder Navigation and the railway company, until the railway agreed to follow canal rates in March 1843.

That was not the end of the matter. Quarrels continued between the parties, with the Aire & Calder Navigation complaining to the Board of Trade about the conduct of the railway in 1844. The Rochdale Company do not seem to have supported this, perhaps because the company was moving towards an agreement with the railway. In January 1846, the Manchester & Leeds Railway Company offered the Rochdale shareholders a guaranteed dividend in perpetuity of £4 a share, which proved acceptable to the Canal Company. A Bill was introduced in Parliament in 1847 that would allow the Lancashire & Yorkshire Railway, as the Manchester & Leeds had become, to take over the Canal Company, but opposition, especially from Aire & Calder Navigation, defeated the Bill.

Trade continued on the canal and on the railway until a form of peace eventually arrived, following the appointment of James Meadows as manager of the canal. He arranged a meeting in 1849 with the Calder & Hebble Navigation (which itself had failed in attempts to lease the navigation to the railway) and the trustees of the Bridgewater Navigation to discuss rate reductions made by the Lancashire & Yorkshire Railway in agreement with the London & North Western Railway, whose direct route across the Pennines alongside the Huddersfield Canal had opened that year. This led to a meeting attended by representatives of the three navigations and the two railways, and an uneasy peace between the parties. This continued for some time, although traffic declined on the canal with a total of 785,474 tons in 1854, and the Canal Company continued to be able to pay dividends varying between £2 10s in 1848 and £3 6s 8d in 1854. Eventually on 23 July 1855, an agreement was reached that from 1 September that year, the Rochdale Canal would be leased for a period of twenty-one years by the railway interests for an annual rent of £37,652. Four railways were involved: the Lancashire & Yorkshire taking a 73 per cent share, the Manchester, Sheffield & Lincolnshire a 12½ per cent share, the North Eastern an 8¼ per cent share, and the London and North Western a 6¼ per cent share. The agreement was sufficient to provide £15,000 a year for maintenance and guarantee payment of a £4 dividend. It was obviously satisfactory to all parties, except the canal carriers who immediately faced an increase in toll rates, although not to such an extent that would drive trade from the canal. Indeed the total tonnage carried showed little variation in the years of the railway lease compared to the years before, varying between 731,141 tons and 878,651 tons. When the lease expired at the end of August 1876, it was renewed until the end of 1891 (although the North Eastern Railway no longer took a share), guaranteeing the continuation of a £4 annual dividend to the shareholders of the Canal Company.

It is often said that the railways killed the canals. Some rural canals such as the Wey & Arun in the south of England closed because of a lack of traffic when a competing railway opened but the main inter-urban and urban canals largely withstood the competition, albeit at the expense of reducing toll rates to remain competitive. What did happen in most cases though, was that the railway creamed off the more profitable loads and carried the huge growth of freight that occurred by the end of the nineteenth century. Had the railways not taken this growth of traffic it is quite likely that the majority of the historic canals we so appreciate today would have had to change dramatically by enlarging locks, bridges and other structures to accommodate much larger craft to carry the loads that were carried by rail. One significant effect of railway competition was that boatmen's wages were cut. Many had little choice but to use their family as crew and take to living aboard in the cramped back cabins of traditional narrow boats. The Rochdale Canal's broad-beam boats provided better accommodation for those boatmen who took their family on board as crew, as they had cabins fore and aft and a box bed and stove. Water was carried in a 30-gallon barrel on deck. A large proportion of traffic on the Rochdale Canal, however, like traffic on the canals of Birmingham, was short distance carrying in and close to Manchester and these boatmen had no need to live aboard.

Throughout the long period of the railway lease, traffic continued on the Rochdale Canal much as before with at least fifty boats moving along one part of the canal or another every day, carrying loads totalling 870,000 tons in 1875. Loads were categorised in a different manner to earlier figures so it is difficult to make comparisons. However, observation of June 1875 shows that a large proportion of boats appear to have been travelling only a short distance on the canal and the majority of boat movements seem to have been largely within Manchester. For instance, of the 25,000 tons classified as merchandise and grain, most loads came off the Bridgewater Canal, with around 4,000 tons originating in Rochdale, 2,600 tons commencing their journey in Manchester or on the Ashton Canal, and only 1,500 tons originating from Sowerby Bridge and the Calder & Hebble Navigation. Nearly all of the timber and 15,700 tons of the 22,000 tons of coal carried that month was taken only a short distance on the canal from the Bridgewater Canal within Manchester or on to the Ashton Canal. So as the nineteenth century drew towards its end, the Manchester and Lancashire lengths of the canal remained very busy but there does not seem to have been heavy traffic to the east of Rochdale or over the summit to Sowerby Bridge. Even so, right to the end of the century most of the manufactured cotton cloth from Todmorden left by water. One boat might carry as much as 30 or 40 tons of cloth, perhaps leaving Todmorden in the evening to arrive at a Manchester warehouse the next morning.

The short half-mile arm of the canal leading into the centre of Rochdale and the wharves and warehouses around the basin there were still busy, as were the numerous basins and arms that had developed off the main line of the canal in Manchester, such as the Dickenson Street Arms, Victoria Basin, the Bridgewater Wharf, the Corporation Wharf, Piccadilly or Dale Street Basin (where the Canal Company had its office and warehouses) which had two subsidiary arms the Flag and Merchants' Wharves, the Brownsfield Arms, the Pott Street Arm, Murray's

Although passenger carrying on the canal ended with railway competition, local groups, such as Sunday schools or the temperance movement Independent Order of Rechabites, hired cleaned-out canal boats for trips, especially on the long level pound below Littleborough. It would be interesting to know who this party were, all dressed up in their Sunday best, and also the man with the enormous megaphone. (Littleborough Historical and Archaeological Society)

Basin, the Prussia Street Arm and the Bengal Arm. At this time, the Canal Company provided warehouses at Sowerby Bridge, Gauxholme, Rochdale (two warehouses and two sheds) and Manchester (three warehouses). Principal canal carriers in these latter years of the nineteenth century also had their own warehouses. Pickford's had long gone over to the railways, but names familiar at that time included William Jackson & Son who had a warehouse and a shed at Sowerby Bridge, three sheds and part of a warehouse at Rochdale and a warehouse in Manchester; the Merchants' Company had three sheds and a warehouse in Rochdale and a warehouse in Manchester; Kenworthy & Company had two sheds in Rochdale; J. & J. Veever had a shed in Rochdale and a Manchester warehouse; Faulkner's had a Manchester warehouse, and so did Marsden's. In 1875, William Jackson took over carrying by water between Manchester and Hull, a service previously provided by the railway lessees.

Not only had facilities developed along the canal to serve the interests of trade but the places through which the canal passed had also changed beyond recognition. This is a chicken and egg story, in which developing industry and trade created the need for the canal but the cheap and reliable transport afforded by the canal then allowed a massive growth in the scale of that industry and trade and in the settlements alongside the canal. Britain had become the world's first industrial nation, with most of its population, which reached 21 million people by 1851, living in towns and cities. Yet when the canal was first proposed the country had a largely agricultural society with a population of around 7 ½ million. Only Manchester and Rochdale could then be considered as towns. Both had markets and Manchester was becoming the commercial and cultural capital of south Lancashire and north-east Cheshire, with the population reaching 75,000 by 1800. The area between Rochdale and Sowerby Bridge was a hive of activity in the textile industry but that industry was largely based in the homes of weavers, clothiers and spinners. However, mechanised cotton spinning in mills, initially water-powered, but soon also steam-powered, was developing in and around Manchester and would shortly spread along the route of the canal. There were as many as fifty-nine cotton-spinning firms in Manchester by 1799, increasingly rapidly to 111 firms three years later. Late Georgian Manchester was seen as a wonder by strangers who had never before seen the new phenomenon of the factory town, or by others as what a French aristocrat and writer on American democracy, Alexis de Tocqueville, described later in 1835 as a 'filthy sewer [from which] pure gold flows'. Manchester had more cotton mills, more factory workers and more steam engines

Working on the boats was a hard life. Ice, thick enough to stand on, froze in these two Canal Company boats at Slattocks. Unable to move, the crews received no pay during the delay. (Littleborough Historical & Archaeological Society)

From left to right: Royal Mill, Sedgwick Mill, the combined block of Old Mill and Decker Mill and Doubling Mill alongside the canal at Ancoats. Old Mill and Decker Mill, dating from 1798 and 1802, are the oldest extant cotton mills in Manchester. (Kathryn Gibson)

Without the canal network, the development of Manchester as a major commercial and cultural centre in the early years of the nineteenth century would not have been possible. In 1825, five years before the opening of the railway to Liverpool, John Fothergill produced this engraving of St Peter's church & Mosley Street. The elegant classical architecture of the buildings and the lady with the parasol were a far cry from any Manchester scene before the building of the canals. (Manchester Art Gallery)

to power the mills than anywhere else in the world; and the growth towards a major city predated the railway. It was dependent on Manchester being at the hub of the regional canal network. The mills developed along the line of the Rochdale and Ashton Canals, at first particularly near their junction where the two canals ran parallel in Ancoats, the first industrial suburb in the world. Here multi-storey spinning mills of up to eight storeys in height were built. After the adoption of power looms for cotton in the 1820s, single-storey weaving sheds lit from saw toothed profile north-light roofs developed on less valuable land further from the centre. With the mills came firms of millwrights, steam engine and boilermakers, warehousing, merchants, banking facilities and rows of workers' houses together with shops, pubs, churches and community facilities. By 1831, the population of Manchester had increased to 182,000, many of whom lived in squalid back-to-back and courtyard dwellings with little or no sanitation; the by-law streets made famous by *Coronation Street* came much later. From the 1830s onwards, areas of housing and industry in the centre were progressively cleared to make way for magnificent cotton textile warehouses, mainly built in a classical palazzo style. In 1838, Manchester justified an eight-paged article by Henry Noel Humphreys in Loudon's *Architectural Magazine* that said the town 'infinitely surpasses Birmingham in the general style and lofty proportion of the houses, and in its noble range of warehouses'. By 1853, there were 108 cotton mills in Manchester and as many as 1,683 textile warehouses for goods in transit or display to prospective purchasers. The fact that Manchester would become a major commercial and cultural centre was apparent as early as 1802 when work began on the Portico Library, built in a Greek revival style, followed by the now demolished Exchange, architect Charles Barry's Royal Manchester Institution (built 1825–35, now the City Art Gallery), and Athenaeum (1836–39).

The growth of settlements was not confined to Manchester. It took place very quickly all along the route of the canal. When work started on the canal there was very little at Todmorden besides a few cottages and the church at a river crossing, with more people living in hillside hamlets than in the valley bottom. By 1802, Todmorden had as many as forty dwellings, a few shops and two or three inns; by 1814 there were six pubs and two chapels in addition to the church. Without the benefit of the canal, a town would never have developed here. It is in such an unlikely place, deep in the Pennines, that even today residents look to Halifax as their centre of local government but have an Oldham postcode and a Rochdale telephone number. When the town built its magnificent town hall later in the century, Sowerby Bridge, Hebden Bridge, and Littleborough had all, like Todmorden, become small towns. All of this was dependent on the new mills, which were mainly water-powered here at first where water power was readily available. However, at least five steam engines were installed in Todmorden between 1822 and 1825. The Fielden brothers, who did so much for the growth of the town, installed a large 60hp engine to power the looms of their weaving shed in 1829. Cotton spread rapidly from Lancashire down the Calder Valley as far

Littleborough and the upper Roch Valley shortly after the opening of railway. Littleborough hardly existed as a settlement until the construction of the canal drained the valley and provided an impetus for the building of cotton spinning mills, the chimneys of which are a prominent feature of this view. (Littleborough Historical & Archaeological Society)

as Sowerby Bridge. As early as 1801 there were thirty-two cotton spinning mills in the valley and seventeen woollen or worsted mills. Woollen mills never reached far up the valley beyond Hebden Bridge.

Rochdale itself grew equally rapidly so that with the combined influence of the canal and later the railway, it became a large industrial town. A new market hall and shops were built in the 1820s, and the town's expansion continued so that fifty years later in 1875, local historian William Robertson noted that:

> The principal manufactures of the town and neighbourhood consist of cotton and woollen fabrics and cotton spinning... Carpets are also manufactured, and there is dyeing, bleaching and silk spinning works. Rochdale is famed for its machinery... as well as large iron and other foundries and steam engine and boiler making works.

Towards the end of the century the town was large enough to offer 'Millinery from Paris', available from G.K. Pelling in Oldham Street. William Stone had two shops selling 'Cheshire dairy-fed ham and bacon plus home-rendered lard – the best for all household purposes'. The Clock Face Hotel offered 'accommodation for commercial gentlemen' and E. Butterworth's Dining Rooms offered 'hot dinners of fresh meat and vegetables daily'. I. Johnson's 'refreshing, invigorating, stimulating, sparkling non-alcoholic Phospherine' was manufactured in the town in competition with Charles Newell's 'Aerated Mineral Waters'. The damp atmosphere of the

Rochdale Canal Company steam-powered flat, Ribble, *under cover and apparently part way through repainting at the company's Dale Street, Manchester headquarters. (The Waterways Trust/ ©The Boat Museum Trust)*

cotton mills obviously played havoc with the muscles of the workers who had a choice between visiting Joseph Handley's shop for 'patent anti-contagious rheumatic flannels' or Bamford Taylor's for 'Sisson's Yorkshire Embrocation'.

By the late nineteenth century, as the extended railway lease drew to a close, it was apparent that the railway companies no longer saw any benefit in continuing the arrangement after 1890, and the Canal Company was increasingly concerned that, without railway support, the volume of traffic would decline, especially over the summit. The company built up a carrying fleet of its own from 1887 onwards, mainly by buying out other traders on the canal. In particular, most of the large fleet of William Jackson of Manchester was bought in 1891.

Until this time, horses towed all of the traffic on the canal but now steamers began to appear, with the Canal Company buying *Grace, Ceres* and *Pioneer*. Soon the company had as many as fifteen broad-beam steam-powered flats but they still needed as many as fortytwo boat horses to tow dumb barges. They also had fifteen short broad-beam dumb barges able to work through the Calder & Hebble to Hull, and thirty-eight narrow boats. The large number of narrow boats showed the importance of the trade within Manchester which went onto the narrow Ashton Canal. By 1893, tolls paid by the Canal Company's carrying fleet amounted to nearly one third of the total toll income of the canal. Tolls paid showed that there were 26,098 boat movements on the canal that year; a marked reduction on the 33,468 movements noted in 1885.

In 1894 and 1899, the company obtained two further Acts of Parliament to allow it to tidy up its financial situation. It had become complicated because the capital structure allowed by the early Acts was now inadequate. The effect was to raise the capital of the company to £752,780, with shareholders being allocated a new share with a nominal value of £1 11s 3.03d for each £1 of old stock that they held. The Act also allowed the company to change its name from the outdated Company of Proprietors of the Rochdale Canal to the modern Rochdale Canal Company. It also allowed the company to sell water. Presumably, this was a tidying up measure to sort out an earlier omission, as the company had been selling water to industrial premises alongside the canal from the very beginning. The steam-powered mills built alongside the canal were sited there not just to take advantage of easy transport, but because canal water could be used in their boilers, avoiding the need for water supply channels, reservoirs and drains. The company had been too adept at maximising profits from its assets to miss this income. Indeed, it missed no opportunity to profit from its assets, even to the extent of taking the opportunity to develop its largest reservoir as Hollingworth Lake.

Land along the shoreline of the reservoir was leased to developers in the mid- to late nineteenth century so that the whole area became a pleasure resort. Thousands of working people came here on excursion trains from as far away as Manchester, Leeds and Bradford, walking up the hill from the station alongside the canal at Smithy Bridge to visit what became known as 'the Weavers' Seaport'. They could hire rowing boats and punts or take the steam ferry to the pleasure

The steam launch that provided trips for visitors to Hollingworth Lake, the 'Weavers' Seaport', with the buildings of the west bank behind. This must have been during a dry period, as the water level in the reservoir is low. (Littleborough Historical & Archaeological Society)

gardens on what the weavers liked to call 'The Cheshire side', although most probably stayed on the western bank where hotels, pubs, an open air dancing stage and a fairground were provided for their entertainment.

Among the larger carriers on the canal at the turn of the century was Albert Wood, of Sowerby Bridge, whose yellow, green and red liveried vessels provided daily services on the length of the canal and also services to Hull and Goole. He had over forty vessels operating on the Rochdale, Huddersfield, Peak Forest and Macclesfield Canals, and from a second wharf that he owned on the Ashton Canal. He also had his own boatbuilding and repair yard at Shepley Bridge, Mirfield, on the Calder & Hebble Navigation. By 1914, the Canal Company's carrying fleet, painted in a livery of red, white and blue, included its first motor barge *Calder* and ten steamers named after major rivers. These had a 25hp engine and could haul two dumb barges together with their own load. That was supposed to be around 50 tons, but rarely could so much be carried. Maintenance of the canal, or at least a programme of regular dredging, although not ignored, had not been continued since the railway lessees took over. The steamers often worked to the docks on the new Manchester Ship Canal or down the Bridgewater Canal to Runcorn, towing two loaded flats back to Dale Street Wharf at Piccadilly. Here loads may have been warehoused for collection or, if they were to be taken east, the steamer would continue alone on the canal, with the dumb barges being towed by horse. But the relatively unchanging world of the boatmen was about to change dramatically as the lamps went out all over Europe in the calamity of the First World War.

three

HE'S DEAD, BUT HE WON'T
LIE DOWN

With the country at war, the government took control of the main arteries of transport, the railways and the canals. Traffic on the Rochdale Canal had been declining before the war and that decline continued, especially over the summit. In 1913, just before the war, tolls had been paid for 25,130 boat movements on the canal, of which 20,635 were for trade on the parts of the canal between the Bridgewater Canal at Castlefield Basin and Littleborough and nearly half of those travelled only the short distance in central Manchester between the Bridgewater and Ashton Canals. Yet the 3,223 boats that crossed the summit level of the canal was considerably more than crossed the summit of the Huddersfield Canal, where Standedge Tunnel now saw hardly any boats at all, apart from the occasional maintenance boat. The Lancashire cotton textile industry was still growing, with a clear differentiation between the spinning mills of the south of the county and weaving further north. Massive new mills were built throughout south-east Lancashire but few of them were sited to rely on transport of coal, raw materials and finished yarn or cloth by canal. Now they depended on the railway and that trend away from the canals was to continue.

As the war ended, with the country stunned at the death of almost 1 million men, and the maiming of a further 3 million from the British Empire alone, there were more hardships to face. September 1918 was cold and windy and the wettest September in London since records had first been kept at the end of the seventeenth century. Many crops were left to rot in the ground. As if that was not enough, the country was struck by an influenza epidemic that killed as many as 150,000 people in England and Wales including my maternal grandfather, in 1918 and 1919. The huge cost of the war had been met largely by government borrowing and the country was in debt to the United States. That debt would have to be paid by higher taxes after the war and they would be hard to pay because prices more than trebled in the years between 1914 and 1920. The country was in no fit state to provide homes and work for the 4 million men

For a time, trade continued in the twentieth century, although at a much reduced level. As late as around 1930, these two boats were loaded at Dale Street Basin. But what was the load? (The Waterways Trust / ©The Boat Museum Trust)

demobilised from the services at the end of the war. Not surprisingly, there were over 2 million unemployed in 1921; a figure that would remain disturbingly high throughout the 1920s and '30s. The phenomenal growth of the textile industry which had provided the backbone of trade on the Rochdale Canal was soon over. The country had continued to rely on its traditional industries of textiles, iron and steel, engineering, shipbuilding and coal mining long after newer industries producing electrical goods and motor cars had developed on a wide scale in the USA and in France and Germany. It simply had not occurred to the leaders of the mighty British industries that the world was changing rapidly and they could think only of investment in more of the same so new cotton spinning mills continued to be built. By the mid-1920s the game was over. In 1926 profits in the cotton industry sank to 23 per cent of their average level in the past five years and would soon become losses as the world sank into economic depression and slump and newer industries abroad with modern equipment and often cheaper labour began to capture the world markets.

All was not doom and gloom, however. Unemployment and its associated miseries remained high but the 1920s and '30s was a time of tremendous change for the majority of people who were in work, changes that their parents and grandparents could never have dreamed of. The ready availability of electric power in the towns

Even the Rochdale Canal Company replaced the faithful horse with motor lorries. A Leyland G-type, dating from around 1920 at Dale Street, Manchester. (The Waterways Trust/ © The Boat Museum Trust)

and cities for new household goods and technologies made life easier in this 'servant-less' age: electric lighting, the vacuum cleaner, the electric iron and the radio that brought universal entertainment and news to almost everyone. Few of these new machines were made alongside the route of the Rochdale Canal as industry drifted south to new industrial estates in the Midlands and the suburbs of London. Even if Rochdale had cornered the market in electrical goods, carrying on the canal would hardly have seen any benefit. A new and much more damaging competitor to the canals than the railways had ever been was developed during the war into a practical and efficient means of transportation: the 'motor lorry', or 'wagon' as it was then known. We would more likely use the American word 'truck'.

Thousands of trucks had been built for wartime service by manufacturers whose names are mainly forgotten today: AEC, Albion, Commer, Dennis, Halley, Hallford, Karrier, Lacre, Leyland, Maudsley, Pagefield, Star, Thornycroft, Tilling-Stevens, Vulcan, Wolseley. Of these, only Dennis remains building buses, fire engines and dustcarts. Wartime control of the canals by government ended on 31 August 1920 but the death-knell of a large part of the canal network was sounded when the government demobilised not just the now unwanted servicemen from the forces but also sold off massive amounts of war surplus equipment, including around 20,000 motor lorries. With the ready availability of hire purchase deals, these were a lifeline to many ex-servicemen unable to find other work, especially as many of them had learned to drive and maintain vehicles or had gained the skills needed to operate a fleet of vehicles during the war. There were few controls and regulations on operation or hours of work and roads were rapidly tarred to cater for the growth of motorised traffic. The motor lorry had an unassailable advantage over the canals and the railways in that it offered door-to-door carriage. The hauliers had to pay only a small annual licence fee to operate their vehicles. That was far from covering the cost of providing roads but the taxpayers met those costs. The tolls paid by canal carriers had, of course, to cover the entire cost of maintaining the waterways. A new transport industry developed almost overnight and traffic on the canals declined rapidly. The 1920s and '30s saw the closure of canals throughout the country. The Thames and Severn Canal, the Grantham Canal, the historic St Helens Canal, The Nottingham Canal, the Droitwich Canal, the Stratford Canal, the canals of South Wales and the Union and Monkland Canals in Scotland all saw their last working boats. The Grand Junction Canal merged with the Regent's Canal, the Warwick & Napton Canal and the Warwick & Birmingham Canal to form the Grand Union, bringing the main line between Birmingham and London into the same ownership and embarked on a modernisation scheme that kept traffic levels up but the scheme was never completed and never paid. No such merger was possible for the Rochdale Canal, and the Canal Company quickly saw that canal carrying could not compete. Albert Wood, the Sowerby Bridge-based carrier, sold up in 1919 and, on 9 July 1921, the Canal Company followed suit, disbanding its own carrying fleet which had been carrying as much as a third of the traffic on the canal. The company was not alone: the Leeds & Liverpool and Shropshire Union Canal Companies both closed down their canal carrying fleets that same year.

Aerial photograph of the canal basin in Rochdale, c.1926. Apart from the tied-up boats, there was little sign of activity. Look at the empty dockside. (Littleborough Historical & Archaeological Society)

Tib Lock (No.89) in Manchester, 1930s. A canal that would once have been busy is now bereft of traffic. (Littleborough Historical & Archaeological Society)

In 1922 tolls were paid on only 8,335 boat movements and only 639 boats crossed the summit; 3,805 boat movements were in central Manchester between the Bridgewater and Ashton Canals and a further 3,553 boat movements continued from central Manchester to places between the Ashton Canal junction and Littleborough. There was very little trade on the east side of the canal. The Canal Company stated, in their annual report for 1924, that trade on the canals would not recover, except with 'government affording adequate assistance, or taking them over and developing them'. That was not an entirely new idea; a Royal Commission appointed in 1906 to consider the future of inland waterways had recommended an extensive widening, deepening and realignment of the major routes that would have required government intervention to bring about. No action had been taken then and it was now too late. The previous year the Canal Company had been so certain that the canal was finished as a major transport artery that they had sold their eight reservoirs to the local authorities of Oldham and Rochdale who were desperate to find increased reserves for their public water supply systems. The Company retained the right to take supplies for the canal from various streams and the local authorities agreed to provide a limited supply from the reservoirs to the summit level, but sufficient only for around the number of boats that had crossed the summit in 1922.

As traffic continued to decline, the tolls paid fell far short of meeting the cost of maintenance. The Canal Company had little choice but to reduce work on an already poorly maintained canal. Trade continued to a decreasing extent at the Manchester end and, to a lesser extent, the Sowerby Bridge end but regular traffic over the summit dried up. What traffic there was on the canal at the start of the 1930s was carried in part-laden boats as the lack of dredging led to the canal silting up. With the bottom too near the top, a fully laden boat would simply sit on the bed of the canal. A Rochdale flat intended to carry 50 tons could carry no more than 35 tons.

The last two loaded boats traversed the canal from end-to-end in 1937. The narrow boat *Alice*, belonging to T. & W. Wells of Wigan, carried 20 tons of wire from Manchester Docks to the Standard Wire Company in Sowerby Bridge in April of that year, and the keel *Thomas*, belonging to Calder Carrying of Halifax, brought a load of chemicals from Manchester Docks to Goodall's Chemicals at Salterhebble, Halifax, in September. The only passage of the entire canal recorded after that was in June 1939 when the keel *May Queen* crossed the summit of the canal empty en route from Stubley's in Wakefield to a new owner, Arnett Grange & Co. in Manchester.

In September 1939, the country was at war again, and the canals were brought under government control once more but there was now no traffic to speak of on the Rochdale Canal. The last infrequent regular traffic beyond central Manchester was carried by narrow boats delivering acid from the Kastner-Keller Company of Runcorn to McDougall's chemical works at Chadderton; from there they continued taking the occasional carboy of acid to Littleborough wharf. Outlying districts in the hills had yet to receive mains electricity and battery-powered radios were much in demand. The heavy batteries for these were recharged and filled with acid at the local 'wireless shop', R. Parry & Sons on Hare Hill Road. Mr Parry collected carboys of acid from Littleborough wharf until the traffic transferred to road in 1941. After that, the canal was no longer used by anyone except anglers and walkers, apart from the occasional boat movement in Manchester between the Bridgewater and Ashton canal junctions; salt to a warehouse at Dale Street and deliveries of coal to the Dickenson Arms for Bloom Street Power Station.

four

RING DOWN THE CURTAIN (I CAN'T SING TONIGHT)

The years of the Second World War passed. Apart from the occasional boat movement on the short length in central Manchester, the Rochdale Canal took no part in the action beyond perhaps providing relief to servicemen on leave fishing or towpath walking. After the war, with a Labour government in power, railways and canals were nationalised. The railways were nearly bankrupt. The large part of the canal network still in railway ownership came into public ownership with them. Although it must have seemed sensible to take the canals still owned by canal companies too as part of the ideal of public ownership, the Rochdale Canal and several others were left out of the equation. The Bridgewater Canal had been owned by the Manchester Ship Canal Company since that large-scale waterway was built in the 1890s. The Ship Canal was considered a port. Ports were not being nationalised, so the Bridgewater Canal was omitted from the list to be brought into public ownership. On the other hand, the Calder & Hebble Navigation and the Ashton Canal, although well past their prime, were still in use and they were nationalised. The Rochdale, however, could not be considered as a means of transport. It was simply left on the sidelines in the care of the Rochdale Canal Company.

At the same time, the first tentative steps were being taken by what would become a major popular movement that would eventually save many of the canals from the destructive zeal of an uncaring world that no longer found them of use. It started with the publication in 1944 of a book, *Narrow Boat*, written by Tom Rolt, an engineer who worked for the Ministry of Supply during the war. The book told of a journey through the Midlands canal network made by Rolt and his wife Angela during the early months of the war on their narrow boat *Cressy*, a converted Shropshire Union flyboat powered by a Ford Model T engine. Few people reading it can fail to be moved by Rolt's sensitive evocation of the end of an era on the working canals and his concern for the future of the canals and the boatpeople. There were too many places they could no longer visit such as the

Montgomery Canal, the Wilts & Berks Canal or the Thames and Severn – all closed to navigation – and even important routes like the major east/west Kennet & Avon Canal were threatened with closure. Perhaps even more disturbing, signs of poor maintenance, decay and lack of use were to be found almost throughout the system. A lock keeper on the Staffordshire & Worcestershire Canal told them that they were the first moving boat he had seen in six months. Rolt received a flood of letters of support, including one from Robert Aickman, a London-based literary agent. In the summer of 1945, Aickman and his wife Ray met Tom and Angela Rolt at Tardebigge on the Worcester & Birmingham Canal where *Cressy*, which had been their home throughout the war, was moored. They agreed that a voluntary body to campaign for the waterways should be formed. In February 1946, at a meeting at the Aickman's home in Gower Street in the Bloomsbury area of London, the Inland Waterways Association was formed, known universally amongst waterway enthusiasts as the IWA. Aickman was appointed as the first chairman, Charles Hadfield as vice-chairman, Tom Rolt as secretary and Frank Eyre as treasurer.

Inevitably, most of the story of the IWA and its battle to save the waterways relates to the nationalised waterways and the struggle to prevent the government abandoning navigation on a large part of the network that remained. It does not concern us here, except to note that the IWA's ultimate successes on the nationalised waterways inevitably had an influence on the Rochdale Canal. Like many voluntary bodies, the IWA proved to be a remarkably disputatious organisation, especially in the early years. Eyre did not stay long. Hadfield soon left to follow a civil service career, becoming the leading waterway historian and founding the publishers David & Charles. By the time the association held its first extraordinarily successful National Rally of Boats at Market Harborough in 1950, Rolt was so out of favour that *Cressy* was relegated to a mooring well away from the centre of events. He turned his attention to writing to earn his living and became one of the founders of the movement to preserve railways.

In this immediate post-war period with the country yet again heavily in debt to the United States, the pound devalued from $4.30 to $2.80 in 1949 and food rationed until 1950, there was no time for frivolities. Austerity ruled and civil servants looked on the abandonment of hundreds of miles of the nationalised waterways as a possible saving that government could make. The LMS Railway had obtained Parliamentary approval to abandon as many as 175 miles of its canals, including the nearby Huddersfield Narrow and Manchester, Bolton and Bury Canals in 1944. Others were soon to follow in the north of England such as the Barnsley, and the Dearne & Dove Canals, most of the Chesterfield Canal and the part of the historic St Helens Canal that had not closed before the war. It can have been no surprise when an official notice was published in *The Rochdale Observer* on 8 December 1948, declaring that the Rochdale Canal Company intended to seek Parliamentary powers to close the canal to navigation between Dale Street Basin in Manchester and Sowerby Bridge.

Three weeks later *The Guardian* published a letter from Robert Aickman strongly objecting to this 'absurd and destructive proposal'. That view was supported by the editorial column of the *Rochdale Observer* on 1 January 1949 but not by *The Daily Mirror*, which on the previous day had published an item, headed 'A Nice Day for a sail round the tripe works!' The publicity was to no avail. A shareholders meeting of the Canal Company later in January decided to press ahead with preparation of a Parliamentary Bill. The meeting lasted a mere fifteen minutes and only three out of the 350 shareholders actually turned up. Apparently, the shareholders now had little interest in the company's main asset, the canal, perhaps because the Canal Company was still making an annual profit and paying dividends despite the almost complete lack of any toll income. The company had made sound investments, it profited from the sale of water and from its ownership of canalside property, especially in central Manchester.

The IWA did not give up the struggle to save the canal. A North West Branch was formed on 17 March 1951, chaired by Stan Offley. The IWA *Bulletin* that reported on the formation of the branch carried an article complaining that:

> The Rochdale Canal is yet again threatened with abandonment, this time, it would appear, at the instigation of Lancashire County Council, whose aim is the all too familiar one of lowering bridges to a height precluding navigation.

The campaign to save the canal was ultimately ineffectual. The IWA had bigger fish to fry in their battles for the nationalised canals and did not have the total support of the limited number of their members in the north, some of whom doubted the possibility of saving such a heavily locked canal when money for public purposes was tight. The Canal Company had powerful support from Manchester City and Lancashire County Councils, who wished to demolish humped road bridges and replace them at a low level. The Rochdale Canal Act of 1952 extinguished the right of navigation on the canal between Dale Street in Manchester and Sowerby Bridge and allowed the local authorities to replace hump-backed canal bridges with new low-level crossings, if a culvert of at least 5ft 6in diameter was provided to allow the water to pass. That mattered because the company was still required to allow the passage of water from the canal to the Bridgewater Canal and the Calder & Hebble Navigation.

What appeared to be the final nail had been hammered into the coffin of the Rochdale Canal, apart from the short central Manchester section that remained in limited use still in relatively good order between the Bridgewater and Ashton Canals. Ironically, a haulage contractor, Wilkinson's Transport, was using the Rochdale Canal Company's depot in Rochdale to garage trucks.

Dr Cyril Boucher, a lecturer in civil engineering at Manchester University who edited the North West Branch IWA newsletter *Nor'Wester*, walked the length of the Rochdale Canal at least once a year through the 1950s and '60s. In 1953, he noted that what he described as 'dismantling work' had begun. The balance beams had been sawn off lock gates and the top gates had been replaced by concrete weirs on the locks at Moss in Rochdale and in Failsworth, Miles Platting and the three locks immediately below Todmorden. The swing bridges at Maden Fold and Moss had been replaced by low-level, fixed steel and concrete structures. After that, every year he noticed deterioration in the condition of the canal and an increasing number of physical obstructions to navigation but the Rochdale Nine, as the central Manchester section became known now that it was all that remained open, was still navigable. Nevertheless, boats moving through Manchester soon became few and far between. In 1955, the Bloom Street Power Station changed from coal to oil firing. Deliveries of coal by boat stopped; the oil came by road tanker. The short Dickenson Street Arms were very soon filled in. Shortly afterwards salt traffic from Middlewich to the salt warehouse at Dale Street stopped too. After that, there was just the occasional pleasure craft but a toll of 15s seemed excessive and with virtually no maintenance the journey through Manchester became increasingly difficult.

Dr Boucher noted that the locks of the Rochdale Nine were in poor condition in 1959 and that year British Waterways excluded the Ashton Canal from the scope of its general cruising licence. Commercial traffic had stopped on the Ashton Canal and its continuation south to Marple, the Peak Forest Canal, soon after the war. Like the Rochdale Nine, these canals received minimal maintenance. Rubbish collected under bridges and at the locks. The two canals were hardly navigable and to follow the story of the Rochdale Canal we need to see what happened to them. British Waterways erected a notice at the head of the locks in Marple stating 'This Length of Canal is Not Recommended for Boating'. The condition of the Rochdale Nine was worse in 1960 and worse still in 1961. The Canal Company would only allow boaters to attempt the canal between the hours of 10.00a.m. and 2.00p.m. from Monday to Friday, and then required 48 hours notice. During 1961, the Hollinwood and Stockport branches of the Ashton Canal were formally closed to navigation and there was a real risk of the main line to Ashton following. The local authorities along the route of the Ashton Canal, concerned that children could drown in the rubbish-filled canal, met and recommended that British Waterways should fill in the canal. Stalybridge on the adjoining Huddersfield Narrow Canal showed the pattern for this. The route through the town was completely obliter-ated and the canal water diverted into a large underground pipeline. The IWA pointed out that the £3 million cost did not allow for providing a water supply to industries that used canal water or, more important, for the high cost of diverting drains from canalside land and surface water systems that ran into the canal. The total cost would be much more than the cost of putting the canal back into good order. To reinforce the point, a cruise was arranged to take place at Whitsun 1961 from Marple to Manchester. Fifteen boats left Marple and, after difficulties with the locks on the Peak Forest Canal, they reached the Ashton Canal. Ten of them continued down the Ashton Canal towards Manchester but they found the gates of Lock 11 destroyed by fire and thrown into the lock chamber. Hardly the work of typical urban vandals but the culprits were never found. Refusing to be beaten, the boat crews manhandled a fibreglass cruiser *Bruce* out of the water, dragged it around the lock chamber and re-launched it in the canal below. The crew, with many helpers from the other boats and with local British Waterways staff helping in their own time on an evening (as they had been instructed not to help in their working hours), eventually reached Castlefield Basin. The canals were now in such a poor state with a heavily silted channel, locks filling with rubbish and lock gates and paddle gear hardly workable that the journey from the locks at Fairfield through to Castlefield Basin took a total of 42½ hours. Later in 1961, one of the Marple locks became completely unusable and a swing bridge across the Peak Forest Canal at Hyde was fixed in the closed position. The IWA held a public meeting in Manchester and sent a resolution of protest to the government.

In the winter of 1961/62, the lack of maintenance led to water seeping into the stonework of the magnificent Peak Forest Canal aqueduct over the river Goyt at Marple. The water froze forcing significant sections of the stonework apart. The Town Clerk of the Bredbury & Romiley Urban District Council (the Goyt forming the boundary between that district and Marple) called yet another meeting of the local authorities but this time including those alongside the Peak Forest as well as the Ashton Canal. Perhaps the lobbying and campaigning by the IWA was having some effect as the conclusion was a request that British Waterways repair the damage and look again at the future of the canals because, without navigation and sensible maintenance, problems like this were likely to recur. The aqueduct suffered even more damage in the following winter but British Waterways repaired the damage – perhaps with an element of bad grace as the local authorities had wrong footed them by succeeding in having the aqueduct scheduled as an Ancient Monument, thus preventing its demolition.

The locks on the Peak Forest Canal at Marple were by this time totally unusable and a leak in the Store Street Aqueduct on the Ashton Canal in Manchester had been repaired by the simple expedient of laying a pipe to carry the water flow in the dewatered canal bed. The IWA was proving adept at lobbying on a national scale but evidence was mounting elsewhere in the country that local battles were best fought locally. In the Midlands, the Lower Avon Navigation Trust had restored navigation to the river Avon from Tewkesbury to Evesham by 1962, and the southern Stratford Canal was officially reopened by HM the Queen Mother on 11 July 1964. Further south, the Kennet & Avon Canal Trust was raising money and providing volunteers to work on that canal; volunteers were also working on the Stourbridge Canal. In 1964, the Peak Forest Canal Society was formed. British Waterways agreed to regular volunteer working parties to do simple clearing jobs but work on the locks was not permitted. The locks were deteriorating fast however and the society publicly defied British Waterways and began repairing the locks at Marple, gaining the maximum publicity for their work. British Waterways did nothing to stop them. The locks were cleared of rubbish, repairs were made to lock gates and paddle gear, and new balance beams were made in the cellar of Dr Boucher's home, which became the headquarters for the working parties.

Narrow boat Parrot *on one of the few stretches of clear water in central Manchester during the celebrated trip up the Rochdale Nine locks in March 1964. (The Waterways Trust/ © The Boat Museum Trust)*

By this time, the Rochdale Nine locks were practically impassable and in March 1964, enthusiasts got wind of the fact that the Canal Company was considering seeking Parliamentary approval to abandon this final section of the Rochdale Canal. To prove that the public right of navigation was still being exercised, Dr David Owen and other local enthusiasts took an old working narrow boat, *Parrot*, through the nine locks to the junction with the Ashton Canal. The boat had to be dragged laboriously along the bed of the silted channel, and the locks were so fragile and leaky that only by making temporary repairs as they went along was progress possible. Lock 85, where monstrous concrete piles, supporting what was then known as Rodwell Tower (now 111 Piccadilly), rose from within the canal and the lock was gloomily hidden beneath the building, was especially difficult. Huge baulks of timber remained across the lock chamber and building rubble was piled up so that even the balance beams were buried. It took twelve days, over a period of a month, to reach Dale Street, but *Parrot* made the journey there and back again to Castlefield Basin.

The Rochdale Canal Company was not easily put off. They could see no future in these locks which, without the continuation of the Ashton and Peak Forest Canals, led nowhere and this was probably the most valuable land of any the canal passed through. The cost of filling in the canal, piping the water and diverting drainage systems might be justified by profits from property redevelopment. The company submitted its Bill to Parliament. Dr Owen arranged a public meeting in Manchester attended by over 300 people that resolved to object to closure, and the Peak Forest Canal Society and the IWA objected to the Bill. The Canal

Company's position was not entirely straightforward. Although the Ashton and Peak Forest Canals were not navigable, legally there remained a theoretical public right of navigation on those canals and volunteers were working at Marple. The company could state that navigation was not possible beyond the Rochdale through to the Ashton Canal, but it could not claim that such navigation might not be restored in the future. The company therefore agreed that it would accept the inclusion of a clause in the Bill agreeing to maintain navigable rights on the Rochdale Nine until such time as the Ashton Canal was formally abandoned. The objectors accepted this and the Act was approved in 1965. So the company had gained the right to close the canal but could not implement that right until British Waterways obtained approval to close the Ashton; it must have seemed to the Canal Company that this was only a matter of time.

In 1966, the IWA held its National Rally of Boats at Marple at the junction of the Peak Forest and Macclesfield Canals, and 212 boats made it from the south through the shallow waters of the Macclesfield Canal, and a further thirty-eight gathered in Manchester on the lower stretches of the Rochdale Nine. Thousands of people were drawn to the event who saw the work of the volunteers on the Marple locks. The Peak Forest Canal Society, recognising the benefits of publicity, followed this in 1967 with a demonstration cruise from Manchester to Marple that took the form of a convoy of boats towed by road on trailers in the absence of a navigable canal connection.

Voluntary work on canals was now taking place almost all over the country. Graham Palmer, of the London Branch of the IWA, was leading working parties to canals in the Midlands and the south-east and producing *Navvies Notebook* recording local canal groups and their working parties nationally so that volunteers could travel to help each other. This developed into what would eventually become the Waterway Recovery Group, a national volunteer co-ordination group that still exists as a subsidiary of the IWA, holding work camps throughout the country. The Peak Forest Canal Society brought Palmer in to organise a massive Big Dig event to maximise the publicity of what they were doing and to achieve an enormous impact over a short time. 'Operation Ashton' was planned to take place on the top pound of the Ashton Canal and the seven locks below that in September 1968. British Waterways had come to realise that the Ashton and Peak Forest Canals would remain a drain on their resources; they might not be maintaining the canals to a navigable standard but they had to do sufficient to keep the water flowing and prevent flooding of adjoining land. Finding no volunteers amongst the local authorities to pay the cost of filling in the canals, British Waterways helped the volunteers by draining the canal and ensuring their staff was around to help. Over 600 volunteers appeared and the organisation was there with almost military precision to ensure that the most was made of every volunteer. Food and places to sleep were provided and dumpers and trucks to cart away the estimated 2,000 tons of rubbish cleared from the canal. As the rubbish was cleared from the canal bed, the canal washwalls and copings were repaired. There was still

Calder Navigation Society and IWA volunteers assist the Peak Forest Canal Society voluntary group in clearing out Tib Lock (No.89), Manchester, on a gloomy day in May 1974. (Keith Noble)

much to do and the Ashton and Rochdale Nine locks to repair, but Operation Ashton was a massive success, and a turning point for the canals.

The local branch of the IWA followed this by organising a conference entitled 'Canals in the Urban Scene' at the University in Manchester in 1970 attended by officers and members of the local authorities, not just along the line of the Rochdale, Ashton and Peak Forest Canals, but also with representatives from other districts around what was being talked of as the Cheshire Ring of Canals. The case was clearly made that restoration of the Rochdale Nine, the Ashton and the Peak Forest to a navigable condition would be the best and most cost-effective solution to the problems of these largely urban canals. British Waterways had a vigorous chairman in Sir Frank Price; he was sufficiently impressed to bring the local authorities along the line of the Ashton and Peak Forest Canals together in a joint working party with British Waterways to consider what should be done.

Seeing the way the wind was blowing, the Rochdale Canal Company suggested that a Rally of Boats might be held in Dale Street Basin at Easter 1971, which was all very well except that the locks between there and Castlefield Basin were now totally impassable. The now experienced Peak Forest Canal Society volunteers set to work on the locks with the help of the Canal Company and especially the company's engineer, Will Kay. The work was heavier than they had undertaken on the narrow locks at Marple, with the problems of larger lock gates and a site tightly confined by buildings and roads, but the volunteers succeeded in patching up the lock gates with second-hand timber held together with scrap signalling rods from British Railways. Although far from perfect, the work was good enough for 103 boats to reach Dale Street for the rally. The Canal Company made their salt warehouse available for the event and it proved ideal for a Victorian melodrama presented on the Saturday night. The Lord Mayor of Manchester and the mayors and chairmen of the other Peak Forest and Ashton canalside authorities cruised through the locks. It was clear that the battle to save the canals was won.

The working party of the local authorities and British Waterways found a formula to share the costs of restoring the canals with the IWA agreeing to pay £10,000 and the Peak Forest Canal Society £3,000, plus the continuing efforts of the society's volunteers. One of the hardest tasks was to dredge the top pound of the Ashton Canal where access was poor and there were large objects dumped in the canal. In collaboration with British Waterways, the Peak Forest Canal Society and Graham Palmer organised a second Big Dig, 'Ashtac' for a weekend in March 1972. The canal was drained and as many as 1,000 volunteers removed 3,000 tons of accumulated debris. When the volunteers left, British Waterways continued work on the Ashton and Peak Forest Canals, and the volunteers returned to the Rochdale Canal in Manchester. With agreement between the Canal Company and Manchester City Council, about who was to pay for the work, the Peak Forest Canal Society volunteers cleared years of accumulated spoil and debris from the canal, and the Canal Company itself did further work to repair the locks. The Minister of State at the Department of the Environment, Dennis Howell, officially reopened the Ashton and Peak Forest Canals with a ceremony at Vesta Street in Manchester on the Ashton Canal on Monday 13 May 1974. The Lord and Lady Mayoress of Manchester and dignitaries from British Waterways and the other local authorities had arrived at Vesta Street by boat from the Rochdale Canal. It was the proud boast of the volunteers to say that they had worked in every lock chamber between Marple and Castlefield Basin.

Fifteen years after British Waterways erected a notice to stop boaters using the Ashton and Peak Forest Canals and ten years after the Peak Forest Canal Society was formed, the two canals were open again after a huge volunteer effort. The central Manchester section of the Rochdale Canal was saved, as the Canal Company's right to close that section of canal had effectively lapsed with the reopening of the Ashton Canal. However the remainder of the Rochdale Canal was not in such a happy state twenty-two years after its formal closure to navigation.

Beyond the Ducie Street Junction with the Ashton Canal, the Rochdale Canal lay derelict and unwanted for a short way, until above Lock 82 in Ancoats where the most astounding action had been taken by Manchester City Council in the name of civic pride and public safety. All the way from here to the city boundary, the channel had been filled at considerable expense with rubble that was then asphalted over to form a long linear paddling pool, no more than a few inches deep. Locks were partly demolished to form concrete cascades, and the towpath was tarmacked and landscaped. The thinking behind this was that such a shallow

Ian Evans demonstrates the depth of water remaining on the shallowed section of canal in Manchester, with Butler Lane Lock (No. 81) in the background. (David Evans)

channel would be safer for the children of Newton Heath and Miles Platting and the intention was to create an attractive linear waterside walkway. Instead, the channel continued to be a rubbish dump but now everything was on display standing out above the water rather than sinking below the surface. It was hardly what had been intended but the work had only been finished a year or two before the reopening of the Ashton and Peak Forest Canals. It was very unlikely that the council would easily or quickly admit their mistake, even after the local government reorganisation of 1974 that brought in new large councils throughout the urban metropolitan areas.

Making the canal shallow in Manchester certainly prevented navigation but it was in theory reversible. There were obstructions that would be far more difficult to resolve further along the line and the many years without maintenance had taken their toll in the derelict condition of locks and the silted channel. The canal simply disappeared into a pipe in the shopping centre at Failsworth, where a newly built supermarket directly blocked the canal. That was the only major building obstruction but roads had taken their toll, as might be expected from the support to closure given originally by Lancashire County Council, because of their desire to replace narrow humped–back canal bridges with new roads at a lower level.

*The canal was completely blocked by the 'Co-operative' supermarket at Failsworth.
(John & Margaret Fletcher)*

*Poplar Street, Failsworth. One of many hump-backed canal bridges replaced by bridges at a low
level across the canal. (Courtesy of Oldham MBC)*

The A627(M) in Rochdale totally obliterated the canal across the motorway terminal roundabout.
(John & Margaret Fletcher)

In 1965, a bridge under Wharf Street, Sowerby Bridge still led to Lock Nos 3 and 4 beyond.
(Courtesy of Dick Booth)

Bridges with navigable headroom had been replaced by low-level structures throughout the new Oldham and Rochdale districts, with another five similarly treated or filled in to strengthen the arch in the Calder Valley. Then the M62 motorway had been built crossing the canal at Maden Fold only a few inches above water level; the motorway continued to the west approximately on the route of the Heywood Arm, so that was effectively lost for ever. A link road between Rochdale and the motorway, the A627(M), had been opened in 1971. Its terminal roundabout and the associated dual carriageway roads were built exactly on the line of the canal. Finally, the road down Tuel Lane to join the main street in Sowerby Bridge had been diverted from Tower Hill to form a new junction near the parish church in 1966. The new junction and the diverted road were both over the line of the canal as was part of the car park for a supermarket so that the canal was piped between Lock 2 and a point beyond Tower Hill Bridge. Locks 3 and 4 were buried.

Despite these problems, there were volunteers waiting to start on another project now their work on the Ashton and Peak Forest Canals was complete.

By 1966, the canal water was piped and navigation was impossible through the centre of Sowerby Bridge. Tuel Lane had been diverted to a new junction with Wharf Street directly over the former canal alignment. Lock Nos 3 and 4 beyond were infilled and the canal was buried under a car park up to Tower Hill Bridge. (Courtesy of Dick Booth)

five

KEEP SMILING

The waterway restoration movement was not the only important opinion-forming group developing at this time. The excesses of 1950s and 1960s redevelopment and mass housing schemes led to a developing interest in the environment, the formation of the national Civic Trust and local civic societies.

One of the earliest civic societies, the Halifax & District Civic Trust, became concerned in the late 1960s about the condition of the Calder & Hebble Navigation which then saw very few boat movements and, especially, about the basin at Sowerby Bridge where the warehouses were disused and rapidly decaying. With the help of the local branch of the IWA, a scheme was produced with suggestions for new uses of these buildings. Although it would be several years before any of these suggestions were acted on, the trust's interest led to the formation of the Calder Navigation Society in 1969. The society became very active in promoting the use of the Calder & Hebble Navigation, especially after a former Windermere launch, *Doreen,* was bought to offer trips on the waterway.

A few years before this the Calder Civic Trust had been formed as a civic society for the Calder Valley, based in Hebden Bridge. It put a huge amount of effort into promoting the idea of a Pennine Park between the Yorkshire Dales and Peak District National Parks to the north and south of the South Pennine area. The trust produced a report, *'The Case for a Pennine Park'*, in 1972, pointing out that:

> The area has much to offer the visitor. Large areas of high landscape value... small tightly knit stone towns and villages, interesting historic patterns to be explored, showing much of the early industrial revolution and offering many historic and literary associations.... [Recreational] developments and consequent promotion of the area would help to revitalise the sagging economies of the valley towns and go some way towards solving their... social and economic difficulties...

This led to the West Riding of Yorkshire County Council producing its own report on recreation in the South Pennines and following that a study of the recreational and tourist resources of Hebden Bridge. Here I made my first cameo appearance in the story of the Rochdale Canal. The county council employed me as a town planner and I was given the task of producing this report. Finding a copy of the report thirty years later, I am surprised that the written conclusions, although not very adventurous, were much less pessimistic about the canal than I recall feeling at the time. The report said that the canal provided:

> An attractive waterway for local rowing craft and a haven for fishermen, and the growing enthusiasm for canal restoration and the economic prospects for recreation on canals now make it possible to plan for the eventual restoration of disused waterways... [The] appearance of the canal is of general neglect with maintenance work reduced to the level needed to fulfil the Canal Company's obligations to provide water. Culverted and ravaged by road widening schemes and with locks converted to weirs... [However] the sensitive development of its recreational potential could restore it as a positive asset rather than a neglected eyesore... It may eventually be possible to reopen the canal fully to navigation, although at the present time certain difficulties seem insuperable – particularly the considerable culverted sections under the M62 and at Sowerby Bridge. However, work is proceeding, mainly by volunteer labour, on reconstructing other disused canals and it may be that sections of the canal can be reopened, if not the entire length. In the meantime no works should be carried out which would prevent its reopening. It is therefore suggested that improvements to the locks, required to raise the water level and improve the appearance of the locks throughout the Hebden Bridge section of the canal, should be of such a nature as not to prevent the eventual reopening of the canal... The road bridge over the canal at Hebble End has been widened and the canal culverted. If at all possible this bridge should be reconstructed to allow for small boats to use all of the length of canal through the town.

This was written only a few months before the local government reorganisation of 1974; the new Calderdale district and West Yorkshire county councils adopted some of the suggestions in the report, but work on the canal would be expensive and not much happened for some time.

A year or two before this, a civic society had been formed in Littleborough, following the pattern of those in the Calder Valley by being called a Civic Trust. Almost from the start, the trust recognised the importance of the canal to the environment in Littleborough. A small group of members actually began work on the canal at Pike House Lock (Lock No.45) between Littleborough and Summit, clearing rubbish from the lock chamber and tidying the lockside. Like most civic societies, the Littleborough Civic Trust held regular public meetings that were advertised with a speaker on an environmental topic. Will Kay, the Rochdale Canal Company's engineer, spoke at one meeting showing slides of new canalside developments and improvements to the towpath at Farmer's Bridge in Birmingham. Before this, there had been correspondence in the IWA North West Branch magazine *Nor'wester* on the possibility of restoring the Rochdale Canal to navigation. The branch chairman, Ken Goodwin, and Ralph Kirkham, the secretary of the Calder Navigation Society, had been discussing the best way forward. They both spoke at the Civic Trust's meeting and took the opportunity to question the future of the Rochdale Canal. Incidentally, Ralph was one of the first, if not the first, person to suggest that waterway restoration had economic and community benefits, as well as benefits for boaters and waterway enthusiasts. The local press reported on Ken and Ralph's questions as an attack on the Canal Company, which might have been true, but did little to advance the cause of the waterway enthusiasts with the Canal Company. Whether at that meeting or later is no longer exactly clear, but the Littleborough Civic Trust arranged a meeting at the Beech Hotel, Hollingworth Lake, that set up a small steering committee to discuss how best to promote the interests of the canal. The Civic Trust then booked a room at the Art Gallery in Rochdale and advertised a public meeting to discuss the canal on 14 June 1974. About a hundred people attended; some from the Civic Trust, some from the IWA, some being Peak Forest Canal Society volunteers, some being local people attracted by the advertisement and a significant number being students from an evening class in industrial archaeology that Dr Cyril Boucher was holding in Rochdale. The Revd Philip Darnborough, a minister on the Littleborough Methodist Circuit and actively involved in the Civic Trust, took the chair. Dr Boucher showed slides of the canal taken on his now numerous annual visits. Ralph Kirkham proposed that a Rochdale Canal Society be formed with a subscription of £1 per person, waving his £1 note in the air. The proposal was enthusiastically adopted and about sixty members were signed up that very evening. Among them was a classics teacher, Brain Holden, who volunteered to take a minute of the meeting.

During that same month Mark Andrew, a Conservative County Councillor on the new West Yorkshire County Council, and soon to be the deputy chairman of the County's Recreation and Arts Committee, who was then the chairman of the Calder Navigation Society, took a hand in the affairs of the canal. He persuaded the Calderdale District Council's Leisure Services department to remove a concrete weir across the channel that prevented boats from gaining access to the canal from Sowerby Bridge Basin on the Calder & Hebble Navigation. The chairman of Calderdale Council's Amenities and Recreation Committee, Councillor Pentangles, prophetically welcomed the reopening of this short length of canal to Lock No.1 as the first stage of a massive restoration project. Mark Andrew was largely responsible for drawing public attention to the historic warehouses at Sowerby Bridge Basin and, by taking a lease of the site, ensuring that no proposal for their demolition was likely to succeed. That had been a real possibility at the time, with talk of redevelopment. He also began one of the first companies offering narrow boat hire in Yorkshire, Shire Cruisers, operating from the canal basin at Sowerby Bridge. An operator of hire boats from Penkridge in Staffordshire was a tenant of Mark Andrew's and built boats for his fleet here. Two of these boats, named *York* and *Rutland*, formed the initial Shire Cruisers fleet.

Even where the canal was relatively undamaged, it was full of rubbish. This is Ancoats Lane Lock (No.82) in the 1980s. (David Evans)

In Manchester, though, the canal was closed again, despite all the work of the Peak Forest Canal Society volunteers. The Rochdale Canal Company said that around £50,000 of work was essential to replace most of the lock gates and carry out further dredging before they could accept an increasing number of pleasure boats. The newly formed Greater Manchester Council could not help find this sum but the council was persuaded to give financial help towards annual maintenance. The company appointed contractors to carry out the work and the canal together with the Cheshire Ring of Canals, was reopened again in 1975.

The Canal Society appointed a managing committee with Revd Philip Darnborough as chairman and Brian Holden as secretary. Philip Darnborough had a charismatic personality well used to public speaking and dealing with officialdom. The society saw the immediate obstacle as the Rochdale Canal Company, who had to be persuaded that restoration of the canal was possible, desirable, and even essential. The company was now very much a property and investment company, and had become a subsidiary of a larger Leeds-based company, Town Centre Securities. The canal was a liability that the company had to maintain and, if it were to be restored for navigation, the costs of that maintenance would increase. Nationally, the waterways movement was finding even the publicly owned British Waterways very difficult to deal with on this issue, and on the unwillingness of the Trades Unions to agree to volunteer work on derelict canals that may take work that their members could do. Members of the Huddersfield Canal Society, which had been formed to promote the restoration of the Huddersfield Narrow Canal two months before the Rochdale Canal Society came into being, spent seven years before British Waterways would agree to voluntary work on that canal. The Rochdale Canal Company proved surprisingly amenable by allowing voluntary work, perhaps partly because of their experience of the Peak Forest Canal Society volunteers in central Manchester, and perhaps partly because of the persuasive powers of Philip Darnborough and the Canal Society.

Brian Holden had been interested in waterways since his brother acquired a half share in a small cruiser on the Lancaster Canal in 1962. For many years he organised boating holidays on the Midlands canal network for his pupils and older pupils had joined in the Peak Forest Canal Society working parties. No sooner was the Rochdale Canal Society formed than he was persuaded to arrange for them to begin clearance work on towpaths and banks of the canal. The society held its first official working party on a cold, wet and foggy Remembrance Sunday in November 1975 at Longlees Lock (Lock No.36), chosen symbolically as being at the county boundary. Indeed the society thought that the emphasis on restoration at first should be on this trans-Pennine section of the canal because of the interest in developing tourism in the South Pennines and because restoration of this section would be relatively straightforward. Working parties continued on this lock for some years until the lock was completely restored. By that time events had

The channel was seriously overgrown in many places, as seen here at Chadderton as late as 1989. (Courtesy of Oldham MBC)

67

The canal basin in Rochdale had been filled in and built over with the MFI and Do-it-all stores seen here in the early 1980s. (David Evans)

moved on and, despite the early involvement in voluntary work and the volunteer background of many early society members, this remained the only lock to be restored by volunteers on the canal.

The society began to spread the word, seeking public support for restoration of the canal by holding monthly social meetings, producing a members' newsletter and taking space at local events and carnivals. Guided walks were organised and a speaker (normally Brian Holden beginning what became almost his second career as the public face of the society) was provided for meetings of other groups and organisations. Dr Boucher, who had been the IWA's honorary consulting engineer since 1965, carried out a survey of the canal from end to end and established that, although there were problems that would involve heavy engineering and high costs to resolve, there were no problems that were insoluble. Armed with this, Philip Darnborough, Keith Parry (whose father had received the last loads of acid at Littleborough Wharf), and Keith Noble (an engineer by profession) met John

Pearce, the chief planning officer at Rochdale. He showed more interest in restoration than they had expected but could promise no immediate help. Ironically, only shortly before they met, the council had decided to fill in the arm of the canal leading into Rochdale town centre. If the council had been aware of the substantial support for restoration earlier, they might not have made that decision, but the prospect of redeveloping the former town centre basin must have seemed a rational modern move at the time.

The local authorities proved surprisingly helpful to the society at this early stage in its existence, compared to the uphill battle some other canal societies have had to encourage even the slightest flicker of interest from their riparian local authorities. Greater Manchester County Council was developing plans and policies for river valleys that crossed district council boundaries. The county council was being lobbied not just by the Rochdale Canal Society but also by the Huddersfield Canal Society, to take account of the canals in this process. Very soon, the county council decided that, if a planning application were to be submitted that was likely to affect the prospects of restoring either of the canals to navigation, they would object to the district council concerned. Shortly afterwards, Calderdale Council adopted a very similar policy for the Calder Valley section of the Rochdale Canal. These decisions were crucial first steps towards gaining official help with restoration of the canal.

The Rochdale Canal Society was making progress that waterway restoration societies elsewhere in the country would have given their eye teeth to achieve but, apart from society working parties at Longlees Lock, there was nothing concrete to show on the canal. The volunteers that the society might have expected to inherit from the Peak Forest Canal Society working parties went away to form Waterway Recovery Group North West, working on sites throughout the country as it became apparent that only limited physical work could be done by volunteers on the Rochdale Canal; something that the committee of the Canal Society had no doubt realised almost from the beginning. The society did not have the money to tackle more than one small scheme, and that scheme would cost a great deal more than the earlier work on the Peak Forest and Ashton Canals. There could be no patching up of lock gates with second hand timber and scrap metal on the Rochdale Canal: completely new lock gates would be required. The whole scale of the restoration effort needed here was on a different plane altogether, not least because of the length of the canal, the sheer number of locks involved and the number of new bridges needed at road crossings, but also because of the magnitude of the problems such as the supermarket at Failsworth or the M62 crossing. The waterway restoration movement had attempted nothing of this scale before, although the Rochdale Canal Society was not alone in facing such problems. The Huddersfield Canal Society had problems just as difficult to resolve with around 1½ miles of the Huddersfield Narrow Canal filled in or built on. The Huddersfield Canal Society was engaged in a process of gaining a large membership and persuading the public, the local press and ultimately the local authorities,

Although many locks on the canal remained undamaged, apart from the removal of lock gates and the construction of a fixed head weir, others, such as Coalpit Top Lock (No.80), were cascaded. (David Evans)

The M62 motorway obliterated most of the route of the Heywood Branch and, as shown, severed the main line of the canal at Maden Fold. (John and Margaret Fletcher)

that restoration of their canal was worthwhile. This would take the Society several years before any agreement was reached that work could start on the canal. The Rochdale Canal Society might have followed the lead set by their neighbours in seeking to achieve a large membership and beginning a hearts and minds campaign to win support for its cause, except for what appeared to the waterway restoration movement at large to be an extraordinary stroke of luck. That clearly was not the case. Quiet and astute lobbying behind the scenes and national events came together to create a situation that saw progress on restoration of the canal while the society was able to remain a small organisation with an important niche role to play in what followed.

That situation came about largely because of pressures faced by the local authorities to deal with issues of decline, depression, decay and dereliction. The cotton textile industry had been failing for half a century, with the United Kingdom importing more cotton goods than were produced at home by the early 1960s. As the 1970s progressed, the pace of closure of the mills accelerated; Lancashire and the Calder Valley could not compete with newer factories in India and the Far East that had modern machinery, were nearer to cotton growing districts and had much cheaper labour. When I did my survey of Hebden Bridge in 1972 and 1973, I found a town that seemed to be dying. It had developed in the transitional area between Lancashire cotton and Yorkshire woollens and worsteds, with a strong emphasis on fabrics such as fustians and moleskins, and branched out into the manufacture of clothing such as shirts or trousers – although keeping clear of the more expensive men's suiting that Leeds would specialise in. There were thirty-two clothing manufacturers by the end of the nineteenth century, with the largest being a co-operative. The Hebden Bridge Fustian Co-operative Manufacturing Society provided corduroys, twills, velveteens and moleskins. By 1972, the industry was almost entirely gone. I wandered around the huge empty floorspace of Nutclough Mill overlooking the town centre and wondered what possible future there could be for the historic building, the town and redundant workforce. The driving force behind the Calder Civic Trust's lobby for a new life based on the quality and uniqueness of the natural and built environment and the development of tourism was only too plain to see. By the mid-1970s, things were worse. In the early years of the decade, jobs were to be found for those willing to move or commute further down the valley. Now the decline extended far beyond the historic heavy industries; it was hard to even get a job in the confectionary and sweet factories in Halifax. Governments throughout the 1950s and '60s had managed the economy to keep full employment, unable to contemplate facing again the spectre of unemployment seen in the pre-war era. That and the attempt to keep up as a world power could not continue because the country paid itself more than it earned. In 1975, inflation reached as high as 35 per cent. After that, it was inevitable that the government of Jim Callaghan should become the fall guys who had to pick up the pieces from the errors of nearly thirty years of economic misjudgement. The government was forced into borrowing from the International Monetary Fund in 1976. Unemployment soared as politicians and trade unions blamed each other and looked for ways out of the crisis.

The Job Creation Programme was a government-sponsored plan for providing work for the unemployed. The idea at first inherent in the scheme was that the jobs created would achieve something worthwhile in the communities hard hit by unemployment. Bill Dudgeon, Rochdale Metropolitan Borough Council's special youth employment officer, like colleagues in local authorities throughout the country, desperately needed to find projects that would create work for the long-term unemployed and unemployed school-leavers. He had only recently moved to the area from London, where he had a narrow boat on the Regent's Canal, so he knew something of the potential benefits of waterways and saw an opportunity in the derelict Rochdale Canal. On 10 May 1976, he telephoned Philip Darnborough to ask if the Canal Society had thought about a Job Creation scheme to restore the canal. It was quickly agreed that a pilot scheme to restore two locks would be developed, jointly sponsored by the Canal Society, the Rochdale Canal Company and the council. Within days, Bill Dudgeon was knocking on Brian Holden's door with an application form for him to sign as secretary of the Canal Society. The amount of money involved, around £40,000 from the Manpower Services Commission plus £6,500 from the council for materials, was tiny compared to the sums that would eventually be spent on the canal, but the Canal Society had no money and Brian Holden was taken aback at signing an application for what at the time seemed to be a huge sum of money for a small voluntary society.

The wheels of central and local government frequently grind exceedingly slowly, but the procedures adopted for Job Creation schemes had to be speedy if any impact was to be made on the unemployment figures. The application form that Brian Holden signed was dated 29 May 1976, the council dealt with its procedures within thirty-six hours, and work started on site on the first Monday in July. Brian Holden recalls that 'on that day, fifty-two lads turned up on site with a cabin for brewing tea and a toilet cabin and nothing else. Only after Philip Darnborough phoned the council did they even have a shovel each'. The council administered the scheme and a sense of order was soon brought to the site near Rochdale town centre at Moss Upper Lock and Moss Lower Lock (Lock Nos 49 and 50), where forty-eight labourers, mainly unemployed school leavers, a small number of craftsmen and their supervisors and a general clerk were under the supervision of Colin Sidaway, an out-of-work graduate engineer. A week later, around 100 tons of rubble had been shifted, the lock by-washes had been cleared and the towpath was again visible from beneath the undergrowth. The remains of the top lock gates were removed and work was soon underway clearing out the canal channel, the lock chambers and preparing for fitting new lock gates. The largely unskilled workforce under the guiding eye of the employed craftsmen, built these on site. The local press, radio and television had a field day;

Work beginning on the MSC Job Creation scheme at Moss Locks, Rochdale in 1976. (Keith Noble)

nothing quite like this had been seen before and the glowing reports of the work gained maximum publicity for the scheme and the canal.

The success of the pilot scheme ensured its continuance, with sponsorship of the scheme, as it entered a second year in 1977, being now entirely in the hands of Rochdale Metropolitan Borough Council. The scheme was enlarged to provide employment for over 100 unemployed people. The Manpower Services Commission would provide £208,000 for the second year and similar amounts in subsequent years. Harry Dearden, who had been the site foreman under Colin Sidaway, remained, now in charge on site. Colin Sidaway found full-time employment. Philip Moxon, an engineer from the Council, supervised Harry but he could only come on site for a few hours a week to check on progress. Work progressed down the canal and they cleared rubble from lock chambers and repaired the lock walls as needed, although the massive masonry of the canal generally remained almost as it was on the day it was built. The channel was cleared out to a depth of around 4ft, with washwalls repaired and the towpath cleared and surfaced with gravel. By 1982, work reached the district boundary between Rochdale and Oldham. The site cabins had been moved several times and with them, the sites for manufacture of lock gates. The whole effect was most impressive, but it was far from being a navigable canal. The council's interest was extending the principles of housing improvement areas, which they had pioneered at Deeplish ten or more years earlier with repairs to houses and a general tidying of the environment to run-down industrial areas. The canal was a central and unsightly feature of the district and the council's main objective was to improve the quality of the environment by turning the canal and adjoining open spaces into a linear walkway-cum-cycleway. The Canal Society lobbied the council to extend the work to full restoration for navigation, but the council's approach was to use job creation monies to pay for labour and combine that with central government Derelict Land Grants to pay for the materials required for the landscape improvements. The Department of the Environment did not consider restoration for navigation to be eligible for Derelict Land Grant, according to the rules then in place. So the canal was still physically obstructed by road crossings, especially the M62 and the A627(M) and, apart from the two Moss locks, most of the locks were fitted with top gates only. These controlled water levels and achieved the environmental improvement the Council was anxious to create. The top lock of the Bluepits locks (Lock No.51) at Castleton still retained its concrete weir, a major gas pipe cut across the chamber of Scowcroft Lock (Lock No.61) and none of the locks had working paddle gear.

Greater Manchester County Council had also carried out work on the canal with a Derelict Land Grant provided for environmental improvements between the Failsworth shopping centre blockage and the Manchester city boundary. The towpath was repaired and the channel was cleared of rubbish and excessive weed-growth, in the process of creating part of a landscaped linear walkway. The Tannersfield Locks (Lock Numbers 66-68) were repaired but the lock chambers were then backfilled and concrete cascades constructed within the chambers. It was hardly restoring the canal but the aim of the scheme was to extend the linear parkway of the Manchester 'shallowed' section. West Yorkshire County Council had also joined in the job creation effort with a small scheme to restore the towpath from Sowerby Bridge to Hebden Bridge.

The Canal Society working parties, under the leadership of Stan Sheasby, had by this time completed Longlees Lock (No.36) and the Society began to hold an annual small boat and dinghy rally on the summit pound. They had continued to further publicise the canal and its prospects for restoration in the hope of extending the job creation work beyond Rochdale and increasing the scope of the work within Rochdale to full navigable standard with a Boat Rally at Dale Street Basin in Manchester on 20–21 May 1978, held jointly with the Manchester Branch of the IWA, and a Waterways Festival at Sowerby Bridge Basin on 28 and 29 April 1979, organised jointly with the IWA West Riding branch and the Calder Navigation Society.

The motorway network around Manchester was slowly extending towards creating a complete ring around the city: the Manchester Outer Ring Road, the present M60. After a Public Inquiry into the route, plans were published by the Department of Transport in 1979 for the final section to the east of Manchester that would cross the canal at Chadderton. No allowance at all was made for the canal. It would be obliterated by the embankment of the six-lane road, with the water flow piped in concrete culvert pipes under the embankment. Greater Manchester County Council, Manchester City, Oldham and Rochdale district

One of the many small boat and dinghy rallies held by the Rochdale Canal Society on the summit pound of the canal from the late 1970s onwards. (David Evans)

councils were all in favour of the road being built. It would complete the motorway ring around the city and relieve traffic congestion on existing roads through town and district centres to the east of Manchester. They were unwilling to risk objecting to the proposals, especially as the Department of Transport and their engineering consultants showed that to accommodate a navigable canal under the motorway would require a diversion from the original course of the canal through a residential area. This would require the demolition of about forty houses.

Philip Darnborough, Keith Parry and Keith Noble met officers of the Department of Transport and their consultants. Looking at the plans it was evident that the diversion of the canal suggested was designed as though it were a high-speed road, and took no account of the manoeuvrability of a boat. Keith Noble, being a highways engineer by profession, could speak the same language as the Department of Transport's consultants and they had to accept that by applying the sort of design standards that William Jessop might have applied in these circumstances, it was possible to design a diversion of the canal that affected no houses at all. With their arguments in tatters, the Department of Transport had to concede that when the motorway was built it would be to a standard that would allow provision for a navigable crossing of the canal. That was only a partial victory. The department had not agreed that they would actually build the canal crossing, only that the motorway would be designed so that a canal diversion could later be built under and around it. The canal would still be piped under the motorway, and the cost of the bridges needed might run into millions of pounds. Until this issue was resolved, the possibility of restoration of navigation between Rochdale and Manchester City Centre remained in the balance, which inevitably affected the attitude of Manchester City, Oldham and Rochdale Councils towards restoration of the canal.

six

THE SHOW GOES ON

On 7 June 1980, the West Yorkshire Metropolitan County Council held a conference on the waterways of the county at County Hall in Wakefield, with an independent chairman, Ralph Kirkham, the chairman of the Calder Navigation
Society. At around the same time, IWAAC, the Inland Waterways Amenity
Advisory Committee, a quasi-independent body set up to advise government and
British Waterways about the nationalised waterway network, produced an influential report 'Inland Waterways – Arteries for Employment and Spending'. For the
first time this gave semi-official credence to the appreciation that leisure use of the
inland waterways was becoming big business. In 1979, recreational users of the
nationalised British Waterways network had spent £55 million, and provided
employment for 17,000 people directly on the waterways and in nearby shops and
pubs and so on. The county council produced a short printed statement for the
Wakefield conference, commenting on the situation on the waterways of the
county. For the Rochdale Canal this said:

> The problems and costs involved in achieving through navigation to link up with
> the canal system in Greater Manchester are considerable but many canal enthusiasts
> refuse to be daunted by the scale of the undertaking. They see a regular programme
> of fundraising and voluntary work achieving a steady improvement in the situation
> and look forward to a happier economic climate at some future date when the
> leisure demand would justify the investment necessary to reopen the canal
> throughout its length.

Buoyed up by the tantalising prospect of a county council that publicly admitted
the possibility of restoring the Yorkshire side of the canal, the Rochdale Canal
Society launched a 'Boats to Hebden Bridge' publicity campaign, pressing the case
for restoring the canal to a navigable standard from the Calder & Hebble Navigation
at Sowerby Bridge to Hebden Bridge, a small town that was beginning to reinvent
itself as a heritage leisure destination, The Pennine Centre. The major problems
of lowered bridge and road crossings, especially the main road crossing at

Fallingroyd and the big obstacle of the Sowerby Bridge blockage, were rather glossed over, and the society (publicly at least) underestimated the likely cost of resolving these issues. If the county council could be persuaded to follow up its interest with hard cash, these costs could, perhaps, be accommodated as a tiny proportion of the rate income produced from the whole county; and possibly government grants could supplement that if the county was willing to invest. The society's campaign was timed to reflect the county council's change of political control in 1981, when a Labour administration took over from the previous Conservative control that had been supportive with local County Councillor Mark Andrew as the deputy chairman of the influential Recreation and Arts Committee. Leeds County Councillor John Sully was appointed as chairman of that committee. Although the Canal Society was not yet aware of it, John was a committed enthusiast for the inland waterways. Within a month of his appointment, he cycled the towpath of the Rochdale Canal from Sowerby Bridge to Todmorden. Seizing the chance of a photo opportunity, he told *The Halifax Courier* that, 'if restoration is feasible we can look for the money', although the county had no money budgeted for the canal.

With high hopes of seeing progress at last on the Yorkshire side of the canal, the Canal Society turned its attention again to the proposed M60 motorway crossing at Chadderton. Although this was to be designed to allow for a rebuilt canal, the cost of realigning the canal channel and tunnelling or building a bridge through the motorway embankment would not be met in the cost of the motorway. The cost of that work, even if it could be carried out at the time the motorway was built, would be high and neither the Greater Manchester County Council nor Oldham Metropolitan District Council could see any way of raising the money. If the canal channel and bridge had to be built after the motorway was built (which seemed inevitable), the cost would be several million pounds. As far as the officials of the local authorities were concerned, that would rule out restoration of the canal from end to end. Oldham council officers were aware of the economic and recreational potential of the canal, but the council was not prepared to continue the restoration work being carried out over the district border by Rochdale Council. Even if the existing motorway obstructions could be overcome (which seemed unlikely) restoration would be possible only for a short distance within the district, especially as the obstruction of the Failsworth shopping centre was not far beyond the proposed M60 crossing. Manchester City Council remained aloof to all of this. Not only did it seem that the canal could never be restored through the Rochdale and Oldham districts to the city boundary, but the council had no wish to stir up the controversy that would inevitably result from digging out the 'shallowed' section that had been completed less than ten years previously.

Remembering the publicity value of large scale volunteer work on the Ashton Canal, the society (chaired by David Marsland since Philip Darnborough had moved to a Methodist Circuit out of the area) persuaded the Waterway Recovery Group and the Manchester branch of the IWA to join them in organising a Big

Dig on the site of the motorway crossing at Broadway, Chadderton. On the weekend of 26/27 September 1981, in pouring rain, over a hundred volunteer navvies toiled away clearing 300m of towpath. It was the only Big Dig that I have attended (not that my efforts with a shovel amounted to much) and I was astounded to see so many people working hard on a site that rapidly became a sea of mud. The council showed its ambivalence towards the canal by lending the barrows and shovels needed free of charge and the Mayor visited the site on the Saturday. A huge amount of publicity was gained and, even if the weekend had no effect on the Department of Transport's motorway plans, the pressure was on Oldham Council to do something, at least about those parts of the canal that were still in water through the district.

When it came to the anticipated breakthrough in West Yorkshire, it came about not through the efforts of the county council but from the district Council. Calderdale had already carried out environmental works in Todmorden that included improvements to part of the towpath through the town. The council was well aware of the Canal Society's 'Boats to Hebden Bridge' campaign and of the possibility of county council support to any work the district carried out. But the real driving force when work actually started on the canal, as with the work in Rochdale, was the economic situation and the very high level of unemployment that now affected the upper Calder Valley. Mrs Thatcher's government had been elected in 1979, intent on putting the finances of the country in a better shape. The Iron Lady may have been right that the medicine was necessary, but the side effects were surely more dramatic than the government had imagined. Inflation was at last coming under control but hundreds of thousands of jobs were being lost. The old industries, such as the textiles of the Rochdale Canal corridor that had been declining for years, were almost shut down with only a few specialist businesses left. The scale of funding provided for the Manpower Services Commission to create temporary jobs, designed to help get people back into work, was increased considerably. The government was looking for a large number of new schemes to carry out work of value to local communities, especially in areas of high unemployment like the upper Calder Valley. It was willing to pay the wages of the people employed on the scheme and pay significantly towards materials and plant costs of the work carried out. Local councils were encouraged to operate schemes themselves and to act as administrative agents for voluntary sector bodies carrying out schemes.

John Thornton, Calderdale's deputy borough planning officer, was called on at short notice to attend a meeting of senior officers to discuss what the council could do. With no more than a couple of hours before the meeting he asked Adrian Rose, the officer under him responsible for planning environmental and regeneration works, for a suggested scheme in the upper Calder Valley, which was badly affected by unemployment. There was one scheme that was immediately apparent that met the criteria of creating a significant number of jobs for unemployed people and delivering real potential community benefits. Frantic phone calls to Rochdale to enquire about the costs of their work on the canal ensued, followed by equally frantic calculations of possible costs and John was given suffi-cient information to suggest to the meeting that the Council could set up a scheme to restore part of the canal to navigable standard. Not only would this create a large number of temporary jobs but it would also have a significant environmental benefit in ridding the valley of its central eyesore and it could help develop the leisure and tourism industry that seemed to be worth investing in for the future of the Calder Valley. Work could start in Todmorden, the worst affected town, with the intention of restoring the canal down the valley to Hebden Bridge or at least so far as the first obstructed road crossing just out of the centre of the town at Hebble End.

Adrian Rose walked the towpath from Todmorden to Hebden Bridge with Canal Society secretary Brian Holden, to learn more about the canal's history and the problems they faced. Engrossed in conversation they walked into a flock of geese. Brian remembers:

> They started to hiss and bite at our legs. I looked around, only to see Adrian had sprinted away leaving me to fend off my attackers. His ability to spot problems ahead and get out of difficult situations were to serve the restoration scheme well.

The county council agreed to act as joint sponsor of the scheme with Calderdale, to second an engineer from their Highways Department and to provide additional funding over and above what the Manpower Services Commission (generally referred to as the MSC) and Calderdale could find towards the £98,000 expected materials and plant hire costs in the first year. Richard Booth, known to his friends in the waterways movement as Dick, was seconded from the county council as project engineer in charge of the project. Calderdale Council leased an old weaving shed at Callis Mill alongside the canal above Hebden Bridge to act as a workshop for the scheme, where lock gates could be made. Nigel Lord was appointed as workshop manager. Work started in April 1982 on restoring Lock No.19 in Todmorden.

Observers of the Rochdale Canal restoration project who have been involved with most other waterway projects are amazed at the political support given by members of Calderdale Council to the scheme. The council changed political control on occasions so there was no continuity of the leading members involved,but throughout the life of the scheme, Councillors have given unfailing support to completing the task they had set out on. Right from the start, encour-agement was given to the view of Adrian Rose and Dick Booth that, if they were restoring the canal, it would be restored to navigable standard. This was a crucial decision that set the standard for future work. Arrangements were entered into with the Rochdale Canal Company over future maintenance so that the MSC team would carry out any repair and maintenance work required over and above those deemed necessary by the Canal Company to meet its obligations for an unnavigable canal. Money was provided in the leisure services budget for this work. I do not know whether Calderdale Council is a particularly good employer or whether it's the attraction of the Pennine environment but an amazing thing about the scheme, after the continuity of political support, has been the continuity of the council officers responsible: Dick Booth and Nigel Lord at Callis Mill, Adrian Rose planning the next moves, his colleague in planning, Alan Taylor (although he did eventually move on before the work ended) responsible for the operation of the scheme and finding grants, and Brendan Mowforth in leisure services responsible for maintenance and eventually operation of the canal.

Maybe we can best get a flavour of how work progressed from Dick Booth's own words, although he does not say that the reality of the early days of the scheme was that miracles were worked on a shoestring budget:

> The initial project was planned to operate with an MSC workforce of about fifty over two years to restore twelve locks and five miles of canal between Hebden Bridge and Todmorden and so enable a trip boat to operate between the two towns. A base and workshop was established in an old weaving shed close to the canal near Hebden Bridge.
>
> Anyone who came into contact with MSC schemes will be aware of the difficulties associated with managing a workforce governed by stringent regulations

Dick Booth (second from left) and a group of MSC workers. (Dick Booth)

designed in Whitehall with the main aim to reduce the jobless figure. In return for this 'free' labour, the workforce should operate on temporary contracts with part-time working and must qualify by being from the ranks of the long-term unemployed. Not the ideal preconditions for starting up a new direct labour organisation. However, work did begin and lock restoration proceeded steadily, assisted greatly by all the original chambers being intact and in surprisingly good condition.

Work on the locks began to remove the old top gates or, in most cases, a reinforced concrete weir, with the flow of water diverted through the upper ground paddles. New cast iron swivel pots were then set into the masonry and anchor plates on the lock top before the new gates were fitted. New timber cills were fitted and anchored to the masonry cill. New paddles and frames were positioned and the gearing either renovated if possible, or renewed when missing or damaged. Assuming everything fitted correctly, the gates and paddles were closed and after a few days to allow the planks to swell, a watertight barrier then existed (at the top of the lock) to allow work to proceed in the chamber below. The chamber excavation was carried out by hand and usually involved about 400 tons of debris, including old lock gates, taking about 3 – 4 weeks whatever the weather. A small

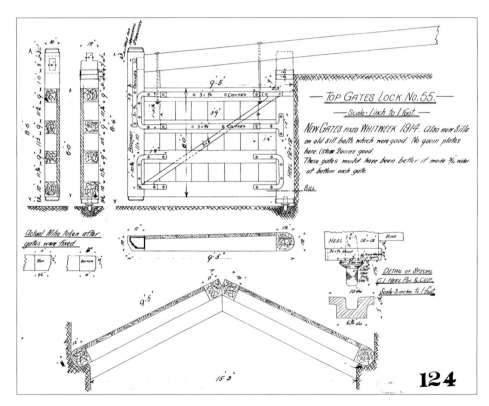

The Canal Company had retained drawings of the lock gates along the canal, which were made available to Dick Booth and the MSC team. These are the head gates of one of the Slattocks or Laneside Locks (No.55). (Courtesy of Calderdale MBC)

Lock gates under construction at Callis Mill, Hebden Bridge. The gates are being routed to enable the metal strengthening straps to be fitted. (Dick Booth)

crane was employed to lift either quarry buckets or barrows which were then emptied into skips, dumpers or stockpiles. The most unusual items uncovered were dummy bombs, resulting in a visit by the army bomb disposal squad. A similar procedure followed excavation to fit the bottom gate, while pointing and repairing the lock chamber walls proceeded. Once the gearing had been fitted to the bottom gates, the lock surround could be completed, involving new fencing, walling and surfacing. Two locks in Todmorden town centre received special attention; otherwise, a natural authentic treatment was required.

It really is an experience to stand in the bottom of a newly restored lock surrounded by 1,000 tons of huge millstone grit blocks, built... 200 years ago. Seeing the individual stonemason's marks on each stone makes one wonder how on earth the navvies built fifty such locks in four years with only hand tools. Fortunately, old drawings were still available for many of the lock gates, which assisted enormously in the construction of the new gates, not to mention the accurate ordering of materials. After all, when 50 tons of English Oak was used per year, wastage was important. Useful notes were found added to many of these drawings e.g., "these gates would have been better 1in wider at the top". Someone obviously thought the gates would be replaced again one day.

Everything was made in our own workshop except cast iron castings and wherever possible the original cast iron shoes, anchor plates and gearing were reused or renovated. Although all the lower lock gates were discovered laid amongst the debris in the chamber bottom, only one set of gate paddle gearing was recovered and reused. Presumably, the remaining sets found their way to the scrap yards.

Removing the remains of the old bottom lock gates from Shaw Plains Lock (No.15). (Dick Booth)

Netting fish before dredging begins. (Dick Booth)

Dredging by hand, including a traditional planking barrow run, was slow and not very satisfactory. (Dick Booth)

A small borrowed monorail that transported trucks along the towpath. The excavator loaded dredged spoil directly to the trucks. The monorail proved unreliable. After it was abandoned, most dredging was by excavator in the channel or by the purpose-built floating dredger. (Dick Booth)

While the lock chambers were generally sound it soon became obvious with use that the walls were not watertight and numerous cavities had formed behind some of the masonry walls judging by the prolonged water emissions from the joints after emptying the lock. In fact after the first trial filling of one lock a long crack appeared in the surface behind the edge copings, indicating movement of the lock wall. Complete grouting of the chamber surround (was) carried out during restoration of each lock and the record was 75 tons of sand and cement to seal the chamber.

The most difficult operation causing most headaches was without doubt the removal and disposal of 300,000 tons of silt. Some sections only required minor clearance work but areas were found to be silted up to a depth of 3 or 4ft. The first task was to transfer fish stocks. Access difficulties and suitable disposal sites created the major problems but operating a fleet of dumpers along a narrow towpath driven by budding Nigel Mansells also helped to turn the project engineer's hair grey. This stretch of canal runs through a narrow valley with a trunk road, the river Calder and the railway all at its floor. The canal is almost entirely bounded on the far side by steep ground often wooded. Much of the towpath side is bounded by the river Calder, and in addition, the towpath is only approximately 8 to 9ft wide with sometimes an absence of any edge protection. Those sections with good access and towpath construction sound enough to support small wagons saw 2,000 tons cleared in two weeks, other inaccessible lengths took several months to remove a similar volume. A common solution was to employ a JCB working from the towpath to load either a wagon or more usually dumpers, with often shovels and barrows feeding the machine across the bed. The most versatile aid to silt removal was found to be a self-drive mini excavator with an overall width of just 5ft and gross weight of under 4 tons. This could operate practically anywhere. Blockages at bridgeholes were quickly removed and direct loading into dumpers or monorail trucks was made more economical. The monorail was a superb solution but totally unreliable.

The towpath treatment was carried out last. A 20/40mm local sandstone aggregate was used as base and surfacing of 10mm pea gravel. Large sections of towpath wall were repaired using old stone kerbs scrounged from the highways depot. Generous grants from the Countryside Commission also allowed more extensive improvements of the towpath and lock surrounds.

The heyday of the Restoration Scheme saw a workforce of 100 and it then became possible to extend the scope of the work.

In 1982, the Rochdale Council scheme, having completed the original programme south from Rochdale, turned its attention to the canal in Littleborough, with the intention of joining up with the work in Calderdale when that reached the county boundary, and at last Oldham Council joined in the Act. Whether the council would ever see a navigable waterway through the district or not, it was apparent that something had to be done. Not only was the canal

The Oldham Council MSC Job Creation scheme begins work dredging the canal. (Courtesy of Oldham MBC)

The Oldham team built a new footbridge on the site of a former swing bridge at Drummer Lane. (Courtesy of Oldham MBC)

Library Lock (No.19), Todmorden, the first lock restored by the Calderdale Job Creation scheme was completed in November 1982. (Dick Booth)

between Failsworth and the boundary with Rochdale an increasing eyesore, but efforts to find new uses for adjoining land, especially the site of a demolished power station at Chadderton by the proposed M60 crossing, might be helped considerably if the environmental quality of the canal was improved. The work would extend the green walkway continuing from the Manchester city boundary beyond the Failsworth shopping centre right to the boundary with the Rochdale district. Like Calderdale and Rochdale, the council saw the benefits of restoration using an MSC scheme, and the council planned their proposals to include adjoining derelict areas, making the scheme eligible for a government Derelict Land Grant. The total programme of environmental works was carried out over a four-year period from 1982–83 to 1986–87. It saw work on the entire length of canal between the Failsworth shopping centre and the boundary with the Rochdale district. The work carried out included dredging which, with the Derelict Land Grant being available, was carried out by contractors and the restoration of locks that, together with the environmental works, was carried out by MSC labour, managed by George Cragg. A Derelict Land Grant of £575,000, an Urban Programme grant of £43,000, a Countryside Commission grant of £10,000 and £2,032,000 from the Manpower Services Commission met the total expenditure on the complete scheme, including works off the canal. The ¾-mile stretch from the obstruction of the Failsworth shopping centre to Hollinwood Avenue, Chadderton, was completely restored to navigable condition, including clearing out and repairing the chamber of Failsworth Lock (Lock No.65). New lock gates made by the Calderdale scheme at Callis Mill were installed here. The 1½ miles in Chadderton between Hollinwood Avenue and the lowered bridge, preventing navigation at Grimshaw Lane, was affected by the council's plans for the power station site at Chadderton and the proposals for the M60 motorway; the only works carried out here were improvements to the towpath. Beyond, to the district boundary, the scheme again saw complete restoration of the canal to navigable condition, including repairing and re-gating Kay Lane, Walk Mill Lane and Coneygreen Locks (Lock Nos 64, 63 and 62).

Meanwhile, the first lock on the Calderdale scheme, Library Lock (No.19) in Todmorden, was complete by the end of November 1982, but with the tailgates fixed in the second recesses of the lock chamber at the shorter Calder & Hebble length. The road bridge beyond the lock had been widened, preventing traditional lock gates with balance beams being fitted at the full length. Rapid progress was made down the valley and a civic opening of the section between Todmorden and Callis Mill was held on Friday 20 May 1983. Dick Booth and Adrian Rose were mindful of the need for good publicity and, loaded with members of the MSC team, a test run was held a few days beforehand aboard a former river boat, *Kingfisher*, provided by Robinson's Hire Cruisers. *Kingfisher* was to be operated for a time by a co-operative until a commercial operation started in Hebden Bridge.

The VIPs disembark from Kingfisher *above Callis Lock (No.13) on the opening day trip to inspect the Callis Mill workshop, 20 May 1983. (Dick Booth)*

After the VIPs had gone, two small boats, one of them steam-powered, sampled Library Lock (No.19) in Todmorden. (David Evans).

There was only a narrow channel in the canal out of Todmorden, as the main dredging effort would follow later. All went well on the test run and Adrian Rose recalls it as 'a memorable experience, with people coming out of their houses to line the canal'. On the day of the civic opening, with the speeches over, the official guests on board *Kingfisher* and TV cameras recording the event, the boat spluttered to a halt almost immediately. *Kingfisher* was aground on a mud bank and the engine stopped by weed entangled around the propeller. Embarrassment was saved by the prompt action of the enthusiastic young workers who, unasked, waded into the canal to clear the weed and push the boat clear of the mud almost before the official guests or the TV cameras noticed anything wrong. All went well after that, as the members and officers of Calderdale and West Yorkshire County Councils cruised down five locks and three miles of newly opened canal. At Callis Mill, the official party saw lock gates under construction and a wooden narrow boat *Seal*, a former Fellows Morton & Clayton working boat, that was being shortened, which included building a new bow section for use as a workboat.

Extension of the original plans was agreed when in November the county council agreed to spend an estimated £50,000 to restore navigation through the culverted bridge at Hebble End, allowing boats to get closer to the centre of Hebden Bridge. The Countryside Commission and the English Tourist Board offered grants towards this work. The new bridge was constructed by contractors using Armco corrugated metal sections to form a tube that was subsequently disguised by stone facing. A continuation of the Job Creation scheme after 1984 would maintain the restoration programme through Hebden Bridge and two locks up to the substantial obstruction provided by the embankment of the main A646 road at Fallingroyd. In Hebden Bridge itself, Calderdale Council negotiated the purchase of the site of Central Garage between the main road and the canal. The county council contributed a further £45,835 to enable the MSC scheme to construct a small canal basin here with an attractive stone paved area between the water and the main road, creating a focal point between the centre of the town and the canal.

In March 1984, Calderdale and West Yorkshire Councils jointly formed the Rochdale Canal Trust to look after, promote the restoration of and use of the canal. This would be set up as a charitable company to act as a vehicle to maximise the use of funds for the canal in ways that the councils could not do. There was an element of urgency because within a couple of years the Metropolitan county councils and the Greater London Council were to be abolished as a means of simplifying local government and saving costs in the major urban areas and to rid

Kingfisher *cutting the tape to open the new bridge at Hebble End, Hebden Bridge. (Dick Booth)*

The new canal basin alongside the town centre at Hebden Bridge. (Adrian Rose)

the government of the so-called 'loony left' councils who did things like subsidising bus fares to cut congestion in Greater London and South Yorkshire. The trust might provide a mechanism for maintaining the canal, which would be essential if the Lancashire authorities were to come aboard. The next objective was the removal of the blockages created by the culverted bridges at Fallingroyd, White Lee and the Moderna works in Mytholmroyd. The existence of the trust enabled the county council to leave behind a financial dowry ring-fenced for work on the canal that would have been lost in general funds had the money been left to Calderdale Council, because the legal arrangements in the management of local government finance would have prevented the council carrying this money over from one year to the next. The county council ultimately set aside £705,000 for this work, and the English Tourist Board also agreed a grant of £80,000. The leader of Calderdale Council, Councillor Eric Whitehead, saw to it that the county council's contribution was matched by a contribution of £500,000 from Calderdale Council to start up the Canal Trust the following year. This proved extremely useful to the trust and the local authorities because it created a pot of money that could be used to expedite things when money was required quickly, something that local authorities find difficult with their need to work to annual budgets. It gave the trust sufficient capital for it to be able to borrow to finance work; something that the local authorities were unable to do, even though they could legitimately pay the interest on that borrowing.

With so much activity, members of the four local authorities now most involved – the two county councils, Calderdale and Rochdale – met in November 1984 and agreed to seek funding to reopen the canal from Sowerby Bridge to Rochdale. Greater Manchester Council also agreed to leave a funding dowry on its demise for the building of a new A58 Durn Bridge at Littleborough. Two months earlier, Oldham and Manchester City Councils had also been persuaded to join the party. They were at least willing to put their names to a joint statement agreed to by the Rochdale Canal Company, the two county councils and all four district councils along the route of the canal. Largely written in the Calderdale planning department with inputs from the Canal Company and the other local authorities, this was headed, significantly, as *The case for the Restoration and Protection of the Rochdale Canal*.

The report listed the arguments in favour of restoring the canal under three headings: recreational, economic and environmental. The recreational arguments were that restoration of the canal would foster the growth of pleasure boating in the north of England, would create two 'Pennine Ring' waterway systems with the Leeds & Liverpool Canal for broad-beam boats and with the Huddersfield Narrow Canal (if restoration of that canal, which had started, was completed), would conserve an amenity of major significance for countryside restoration, and would protect a long-distance footpath route providing a direct link between major urban areas and the Pennines. The economic argument said that restoration would result in new employment, managing and maintaining the canal and in new businesses directly linked to the canal such as boat hire, boat repair, trip boats and restaurant boats. A restored canal would create new confidence in canalside property and attract investment, not just in businesses with direct waterway links such as boat repair or pubs and restaurants, but also simply as a response to the improved environmental quality. Restoration of the canal would also be a major attraction in stimulating the growth of tourism that could play an important role in the economic regeneration of the area. Environmentally, restoration of the canal would transform an area of dereliction from being a neglected backwater and a public danger into an asset for the communities along its route but only if it was restored to a navigable standard ensuring its future use and maintenance. Restoration would conserve a feature of outstanding industrial archaeological significance and would protect an amenity of special natural history interest.

The local authorities and the Canal Company set out what were called their statements of intent. The Canal Company would continue to fulfil its statutory obligations in respect of the canal but it would also support initiatives leading to restoration. The local authorities would protect the route from further infilling or building and would continue their initiatives to improve sections of the canal, while seeking to restore the canal to navigable standards 'where realistic possibilities arise'. The statement was very important because for the first time the Canal Company put its support of restoration in writing, and also, for the first time all of the local authorities along the canal were involved. The sting however, was in those weasel words in the tail 'where realistic possibilities arise', and the local authorities on the Lancashire side of the canal would continue to shelter behind them as long as the threat of the route being split for all time by the M60 motorway existed.

On the Yorkshire side, however, progress continued, not just by Dick Booth and the MSC scheme, but also by Calderdale Council planning for ultimate complete restoration of the canal to the county boundary and connection to the national waterway network at Tuel Lane, Sowerby Bridge. In January 1985, the Council decided to buy the disused Regent Cinema in Sowerby Bridge. The canal had been filled in behind the building, and the site would provide space to relocate car parking that would be lost when the canal was rebuilt behind the shops in the town centre. The council was also seriously looking at how the reconnection to the Calder & Hebble Navigation could be made; officers even considered the possibility of creating a link to the river Calder and canalising the river as an alternative to building an expensive cut-and-cover tunnel under the new roads. British Waterways was asked for its views and reported that this was not a feasible solution. It would require excavation of the riverbed to provide navigable depth, the construction of expensive weirs and lock cuts on the river and the raising of road bridges, not to mention having a dramatic effect on the ecology and hydraulic regime of the river Calder and its tributary, the Ryburn. Whatever route was followed at Sowerby Bridge, the district council was increasingly worried that the abolition of the county council would seriously affect the funding of and the pace of restoration. The county council had produced engineering drawings showing how the canal could be reconnected to the Calder & Hebble navigation by a cut-and-cover tunnel under the roads, but the cost would be high and difficult for the district council to find, unless significant grants were obtained.

In June 1985, Calderdale Council adopted a programme of work leading toward complete restoration of the canal in the Calder Valley. The work on new bridges at Fallingroyd, White Lee and Moderna would be completed in 1986. These works would be followed by restoration of the canal through the car park area in Sowerby Bridge to create a turning space before the road obstruction, reconstruction of Longbottom's Bridge between Sowerby Bridge and Luddenden Foot and restoration of the canal beyond Todmorden to the county boundary including the building of a new main road bridge at Copperas House, Walsden. It was just possible for all of this work to be completed before 1990 even without further funding from the county council, but only in the unlikely events of the council achieving 100 per cent success in the various grant applications that might be made and in there being no unforeseen problems. We know that it is not uncommon for public works and works affecting historic structures to be subject to unforeseen problems especially where, as in canal restoration, there are hidden features underground or underwater. To help pay for this work the council submitted bids for grants, especially for a European Regional Development Fund grant.

A most encouraging sign that the renaissance of the canal in the Calder Valley was not just cosmetic occurred in the summer of 1985. Shire Cruisers of Sowerby

Rochdale Pioneer *is launched by crane at Hebden Bridge, summer 1985. (Dick Booth)*

Bridge, now owned by Nigel Stevens who had earlier been involved with the London & Home Counties branch of the IWA and the Waterway Recovery Group, put a modern steel hire narrow boat, aptly named *Rochdale Pioneer,* on the canal at Hebden Bridge. County Councillor John Sully and his family were the first hirers. With only six miles of canal between Hebden Bridge and Todmorden available, this was a very brave step but it was justified by success. The boat was hired out not just to waterway enthusiasts seeking to try a new waterway experience but also by a growing number of people interested in the industrial and architectural heritage of the area and the countryside, for whom the boat provided an ideal moving base, and to families in search of a simpler holiday than those provided by foreign package holidays. In Hebden Bridge, Calder Cruisers' trip boat *Sarah Siddons* was operating, towed by its tug, *Oliver.* Indeed the canal was proving so popular that the Canal Trust, which had taken over responsibility for boat licenses from the Canal Company, had issued twenty-one licenses by the end of 1986.

Brian Holden, the Canal Society's secretary, was so inspired by the progress of restoration down the Calder Valley and the attitude of the Calderdale and West Yorkshire Councils that he told *Waterways World* magazine that 'even if the Canal Society folded tomorrow, restoration would continue'. That may have been an exaggeration but, at the time, it seemed that it might have turned out to be true if only the threat of the proposals for the M60 motorway was not still hanging over the Lancashire side of the canal. After the euphoria of progress on the canal and

Rochdale Pioneer *proved so popular with hirers that it was soon joined by a second boat,* Rochdale Progress. *(David Evans)*

*Private boats also began to be based on the restored canal. Here a boat is craned in at Walsden.
(David Evans)*

the decisions made for future restoration in 1984 and 1985, the Department of Transport's announcement of its detailed plans for the Manchester Outer Ring Road brought everyone involved in the canal scheme down to earth with a very heavy bump in May 1985.

The Minister of State for Transport, Lynda Chalker, said in a press release:

> Among the many issues we have had to consider is the treatment of the disused Rochdale Canal near Chadderton. Many people have asked us to provide a navigable crossing there so as not to present another obstacle to the future restoration of through navigation. However, we conclude that the existing obstructions on the canal south of Rochdale – including existing motorways and major roads, a supermarket and the shallowed length near the centre of Manchester – effectively rule out restoration of through navigation. We could not, therefore, justify spending over £2m extra on providing for navigation.

The society, the local authorities and the Canal Company had to turn their attention to the Public Inquiry into the motorway that was planned to take place in 1986. The result was far from certain – indeed had bookmakers taken bets, the Department of Transport would have been the clear favourite.

seven

LOOKING ON THE BRIGHT SIDE

As 1986 dawned bright, but very cold, the Rochdale Canal Society had reasons to be optimistic that work taking place or planned would eventually see the canal restored between Littleborough and Sowerby Bridge. Not only were the Rochdale and Calderdale MSC teams making good progress but work was in hand on new bridge crossings at White Lee, Fallingroyd and Durn Bridge, funded largely by the two county councils, and the Calderdale MSC team was about to build another bridge access to the Moderna industrial estate at Mytholmroyd. Between Littleborough and Manchester was a different story however, blighted by lowered and culverted bridges preventing navigation, the supermarket across the line of the canal at Failsworth, the shallowed section in Manchester and the plans for the M60 motorway.

Rochdale Council had carried out significant improvements between Rochdale and the district boundary with Oldham but that work was in reality only cosmetic; the locks had not been restored to a navigable state and would need further work. Eight new bridges, where the water was piped in culverts under roads, would be needed between Littleborough and the boundary with the Oldham district. Then there were the large-scale works required at the A627(M) roundabout and the M62. Work on the canal in the Oldham district was restoring the canal to a navigable condition between the Failsworth shopping centre and the Rochdale boundary, apart from the long section affected by the proposals for the Broadway Business Park and the M60 crossing that remained heavily silted and included a culverted bridge at Grimshaw Lane. Then there was the major problem of the Failsworth shopping centre itself and, close to that, the Haweswater Aqueduct, a major water pipe delivering water from the Lake District to Manchester that crossed the canal with no headroom for boats. Lowered and culverted bridges at Ashton Road West and Poplar Street followed, and the three cascaded Tannersfield Locks (Lock Numbers 66, 67 and 68) before the Manchester boundary and the long shallowed section. The shallowed section itself would be difficult and

98

The winter of 1985/86 saw the canal freeze over; the dredger built at Callis Mill proved its abilities as an icebreaker, even if actual dredging work had to be postponed until the thaw. (Dick Booth)

expensive to remedy and included another thirteen part-demolished and cascaded locks. It was evident that as long as the blighting effect of the M60 proposals remained, there were no prospects of the Lancashire district councils considering how to tackle these obstructions to navigation and, even if the M60 plans could be overcome, restoration between Littleborough and Manchester would be difficult to achieve.

Although Manchester City, Oldham and Rochdale District Councils and Greater Manchester County Council had joined with Calderdale and West Yorkshire Councils and the Rochdale Canal Company in putting their names to 'The Case for the Restoration and Protection of the Rochdale Canal' in 1984, and work was taking place on the canal, the three Lancashire District Councils could not make the major commitments to restoration seen in Yorkshire. Greater Manchester County Council's commitment was shown by the work taking place to build a new navigable Durn Bridge at the A58 road crossing in Littleborough, but the county councils were to be abolished at the end of March 1986 and with them the only likely source of funding to begin to tackle the other obstructions to navigation in Lancashire. The problems facing the three Lancashire District Councils were difficult to solve unless the councils could raise the money either from their own resources or from grants to tackle the obstructions to navigation in an incremental way. That would have been a logical way of knocking off the problems one-by-one, starting with the Ben Healey Bridge crossing in

Littleborough but could they or any likely grant-aiding bodies justify spending a large sum of money on even the first project in such an incremental approach when there were so many other obstructions to tackle and these were so evenly spread that only small environmental benefits would accrue from simply tackling one or two obstacles?

Dates were fixed for the Public Inquiry into the motorway, which would last throughout the summer of 1986 at the Civic Centre in Oldham. An Inspector was appointed, Sir Michael Giddings, who would hear the evidence and make recommendations to the Departments of Environment and Transport on whether the motorway should be allowed as planned, or if it needed modifications. Major public inquiries have a format whereby the party proposing the works (in this case the combined government Departments of Transport and the Environment) and the major opponents to a proposal are represented by a solicitor or barrister who leads their case and calls expert witnesses to give evidence to the inquiry. The cost of such legal representation was way beyond the means of the Rochdale Canal Society. David Marsland, the chairman of the society, approached the IWA for help. Michael Handford, the chairman of the IWA's Restoration Committee, had taken considerable interest in the issue of road crossings of derelict and disused waterways. He probably knew more about the subject than anyone outside of the Department of Transport did. He was a Midlands-based lecturer in travel and tourism studies, who had carried out consultancy work and given advice and help to numerous waterway schemes throughout the country, including giving evidence at Public Inquiries. Michael decided that he would lead a combined Canal Society and IWA case against the motorway crossing. Whatever apprehension he felt at taking on the might of the government machine he wisely kept to himself, and he kept up an appearance of confidence that the case for the canal was irrefutable. His only stipulations were that the canal-related evidence should be presented to the inquiry out of term-time and that the IWA and the Canal Society should pay his expenses.

It was crucial to the case that the Canal Society and the IWA would put forward that the three Lancashire District Councils join with the Canal Society and Calderdale Council in opposing the lack of a navigable canal crossing at the M60 motorway. Unless the councils joined in the opposition, the case would almost inevitably be lost and the new motorway would sever the canal. The councils were firmly in favour of the motorway. It would improve access to their districts, which could help them to attract investment that would create desperately needed new jobs and it would relieve traffic congestion on existing main roads. The three councils were concerned that if they objected to the proposals for the canal crossing too vehemently, the extra costs involved might scupper the motorway proposal.

Calderdale Council officers and members and the Canal Society went into persuasion overdrive. I doubt that we will ever know how they achieved it, but before the Public Inquiry began, Oldham and Rochdale Councils had both decided that the greater benefit for their communities would be achieved if they could somehow find the money to restore the canal to navigation. The two councils decided that they could support the principle of the motorway while at the same time objecting to the detail of the canal crossing and that they would join with Calderdale Council and the Canal Company as members of the Rochdale Canal Trust. Manchester City Council was a harder nut to crack, and the Inquiry began with that council remaining outside of the canal restoration partnership: it was an understandable view perhaps because of the difficulties to be overcome in Rochdale and Oldham before restoration in Manchester was worthwhile.

The Public Inquiry began on 8 April 1986. The Lancashire local authorities were represented by their solicitors each calling his own witnesses with evidence on the principle of supporting the road but Calderdale, Oldham and Rochdale needed to present a united front with the case being put by the Canal Society and the IWA. They saw this as best presented as a separate issue. It was evident that the IWA in particular could make comparisons with similar issues elsewhere and it would do the councils' case no harm to be associated with the voluntary sector that could make something of the iniquity of volunteers having to fight the mighty Department of Transport. Soon Michael Handford found that he was presenting the case for all of the objectors to the obstruction of the canal: the Canal Society and the IWA, the local authorities and the Rochdale Canal Trust, the Rochdale Canal Company, the Association of Pleasure Craft Operators and numerous private individuals objecting to the plans. The councils offered help and provided witnesses but Brian Holden found that he had to fill the role that a local authority would have provided an administrative assistant for: shepherding the witnesses to ensure that the right person turned up at the right time and ensuring that Michael Handford had the information he needed at the time he needed it. The major missing items in this information to present to the Inquiry were independent evidence of the likely costs of removing or otherwise over-coming all of the obstructions to navigation to prove that the total cost was not quite as high as might be feared and an independent study of the benefits likely to result from the restoration of the canal. A combination of these two pieces of information would, all being well, show that the benefits of restoring the canal from end to end outweighed the costs of carrying out the work. Financial help from the local authorities and the Canal Society allowed the IWA to appoint engineering and economic consultants W.S. Atkins and Partners to carry out this study.

The Inspector, Sir Michael Giddings, agreed that the canal evidence could be heard in three phases. First of all the local authorities and the Canal Society were allowed to show him the canal, the work already carried out, the work being carried out or planned, and the existing obstructions to navigation as part of his site inspection of the route of the motorway. The main body of the canal-related evidence was heard in the early summer holiday period when Michael Handford was available but the results of the Atkins study would not be ready until autumn. The Inspector agreed to return to the subject of the canal then.

The M60 motorway Public Inquiry Inspector, Sir Michael Giddings, inspecting the canal in Manchester. (John and Margaret Fletcher)

Sir Michael Giddings spent four days looking at the canal. He was very thorough, looking at everything between Castlefield Basin and Sowerby Bridge in detail. It was pointed out that measured by length, nearly one third of the canal was already fully restored and one third partially restored or planned. To back up their campaign, the Rochdale Canal Society and the IWA held a protest rally on the canal at Chadderton on 26 April, where it would be blocked by the motorway to coincide with the beginning of the Inquiry. Warm sunshine greeted the hundreds of spectators who came to see the thirty or so boats that were craned in for the occasion, including a narrow boat and trailable cruisers. The Calder Navigation Society's *Doreen* and the Huddersfield Canal Society's *Stan* gave short public trips on the canal.

When the time came to present the canal evidence, Michael Handford told the inspector that the parties he represented had no objection to the principle of building the motorway, indeed the Lancashire local authorities had all separately presented evidence of their support. The objection he was presenting was to 'the disastrous impact this motorway, as it is currently designed, will have on the restoration of the Rochdale Canal after millions of pounds of taxpayers' and ratepayers' money has already been spent on renovating it'. He said: 'We are not asking anyone to restore the canal. We are asking the Minister not to leave the canal at the end of construction in a worse state than it is now'. There was a national revival of canals as a major recreational asset, creating substantial economic and social benefits for the areas through which they pass, and a national trend for

Boats on the canal at Chadderton, M60 Protest Rally, April 1986. (John and Margaret Fletcher)

the restoration of previously unnavigable waterways using a combination of voluntary labour and public sector funding. Indeed, there were over seventy restoration schemes underway or proposed in the UK, including others affected by similar highway proposals where the Department of Transport showed the inconsistency of its planning. A new bridge was being built for the A5 by-pass at Oswestry, where that road would cross the derelict Montgomery Canal. Of the seventy schemes he had identified, the Rochdale Canal had made the most progress in recent times; it was a canal of national rather than purely local signifi-cance. The canal had been championed by 'an unusually persuasive canal society' that had been so successful that 'the restoration has been totally taken over by the MSC and local authorities'. The trend of progress on the canal pointed 'very strongly to continued restoration into the more difficult section. No restoration I know of has ever given up halfway with this degree of support'. Over £10 million of public money had already been spent on the canal and the 'political will' was there to see that the money needed to complete restoration would eventually be found. The Department of Transport was 'isolated' in its view that restoration was 'a vague hope'; none of the local authorities, landowners, local residents, and amenity groups, councillors, businessmen, tourist boards, MPs and so on supported the plan to pipe the canal under the road. 'You cannot take a thirty-two mile canal, decide policy for eight hundred and odd metres of it on its own, without serious – correction, without *any* – consideration of what this insular and narrow decision will have on the remaining substantial mileage'.

He pointed out the reasons for restoration given in *The Case for the Restoration and Protection of the Rochdale Canal* and said that:

> The position now is that local authorities and other fund providers are removing the mistakes of the 1960s and early 1970s on the canal. They are spending money removing blockages they now recognise they should not have supported and wish now they never had... The lessons have been learned by everyone but the Department of Transport. They propose that everyone else should have to pay for removing that blockage when restoration reaches Chadderton. Local authorities oppose the new blockage because they know from hard experience of reaching deeply into their pockets... A decision to build the motorway and pipe the canal would not stop restoration of the canal but it would make it much, much harder. Would such a decision assist Calderdale Metropolitan Borough Council assemble the funds to remove the blockage at Tuel Lane, Sowerby Bridge? It would not. Would it dampen the commitment, drive and sheer effort of all the local authorities and demoralise the huge range of community organisations which support this? The potential damage and discouragement this proposed economic, social and environmental vandalism would probably have should be enough to turn it down on those grounds alone.

The total restoration cost to remove the remaining obstructions to navigation would be high but sources of funding from European and central government grants existed so that, with a continuation of the MSC schemes, in time problems could be overcome. Finally, he asked if the Department of Transport had considered the expense involved in fighting this issue, with around three weeks of expensive professional and legal time involved for the canal element of the Inquiry, let alone the time preparing the evidence. The Canal Society estimated that this had probably cost more than the extra cost of providing a navigable culvert.

The local authority witnesses gave their views in support of the case with the triumvirate of planners: Adrian Rose, John Billington and Andrew Swaby from Calderdale, Oldham and Rochdale, co-ordinating their evidence in support of the canal. John Billington, for Oldham Council, for instance, explained the work the council had already carried out and planned to carry out. He referred in detail to the benefits that restoration would bring to the communities alongside the canal, split into categories: recreational, environmental and economic. He said:

> Although the council accepts that partial restoration of the canal is in itself desirable, it is convinced that the full economic, recreational and environmental benefits will only result when through navigation is achieved. There is evidence in Manchester and Failsworth that environmental improvements alone are not sufficient to ensure the future of the waterway or to achieve major benefits... Depositing of rubbish and vandalism continue to be problems and add to the maintenance burden of local authorities. However, if through restoration can be achieved, the council believes

that the canal will become a major recreational amenity of regional as well as local importance; it will create employment on and around the canal; it will attract new uses for land and property and it will attract people and income to the area to help regenerate the local economy. [The council felt] that the current proposals would not only add to the eventual cost of restoration but are in conflict with both central and local government policies towards canal restoration and make a nonsense of the large central and local government investments already made.

For the Canal Society, David Marsland was a particularly strong witness, playing on the Society's David v. Goliath position in regard to the Department of Transport. He was one of many other witnesses called, so widely had the Canal Society and the IWA drawn their net of support. Other witnesses represented: the IWA, the Canal Company, the Rochdale Canal Trust, British Waterways, the Association of Pleasure Craft Operators, Littleborough Heritage Centre, the Ship and Boat Builders' Federation, the National Waterways Museum, the Yorkshire and Humberside Council for Sport and Recreation, the North West Tourist Board, Todmorden Town Council, the Slattocks and District Community Association, the Oldham and Rochdale Groundwork Trust, the Rochdale Civic Society, the Middleton Civic Association, the Sowerby Bridge Civic Society, the Failsworth Amenity Society, the Chadderton Historical Society, the Saddleworth Historical Society, the Littleborough Historical & Archaeological Society, the Chesterfield Canal Society, Pennine Heritage, the Oldham and District Historical & Antiquarian Society, the North West Sports Council, the Sowerby Bridge Chamber of Trade, Shire Cruisers, the Calder Navigation Society and the Calder Civic Trust. Even I appeared, making my third cameo appearance in the story of the Rochdale Canal, representing the Huddersfield Canal Society to give support to our neighbours and to say that we were concerned that the economic benefits of restoring the Huddersfield Narrow Canal might be reduced if the Rochdale Canal was not completed to create a 'Pennine Ring' of canals. Several individuals gave evidence, including ex-County Councillors John Sully and Allen Brett. Allen was also a member of Rochdale Council representing the Milnrow ward.

When the Inquiry returned to the subject of the canal in October, Jim Saunders of consultants W.S. Atkins, and his colleagues Dr Fletcher and Dr Bell, gave evidence of the findings of their study. They presented drawings of their proposals for major issues such as the A627(M) crossing and Failsworth shopping centre. They concluded that the cost of full restoration of the canal would be around £10 million, assuming the continued availability of MSC labour. This restoration was likely to result in £3.7 million of additional spending in the region by tourists and the creation of around 227 full time jobs directly from that additional expenditure. Even without taking account of other benefits likely to accrue such as new investment attracted by the canalside environment and the resulting jobs that might bring, or the increase in property values and the importance of the canal as a local amenity, restoration of the canal was justified. If the M60 motorway were allowed to bisect the canal, however, there would be a very limited demand for boating use of the severed Manchester length. Cruising use of the remainder of the canal would be substantially less than the levels of use likely from a completely restored canal, thus reducing the possible benefits gained by the canalside communities. This would be especially the case on the Lancashire section, as few boaters would venture far beyond the summit.

The clear evidence that Jim Saunders and his colleagues presented to the inquiry showed that restoration beyond Failsworth shopping centre and the cost and upheaval of creating a new canal route through that site was unlikely ever to happen without the involvement of Manchester City Council. There would be little point in Oldham Council finding the large sums needed to build a new route through Failsworth, and the compensation and land costs needed over and above the construction costs, if the canal remained as a shallow linear paddling pool through Newton Heath and Miles Platting. Indeed, if boaters had to turn at Failsworth, perhaps the Department of Transport's accusation that complete restoration of the canal was no more than a 'vague hope' was true and the extra mile of navigable water available between Failsworth and the proposed motorway crossing was simply not worth the cost of providing a navigable crossing at the motorway. Throughout the summer, lobbying of Manchester City Councillors and officers was intense, now strengthened by the addition of pressure from Oldham and Rochdale. Again, we will never know how it was achieved – for instance, what Oldham Councillors Jacobs and Greenwood may have said to their counterparts on Manchester City Council – but it was achieved. Manchester City Council was aware that the linear paddling pool had been far from the desired success. The sad tendency to dispose of the detritus of modern living in the nearest place was only too apparent in water too shallow to hide even a beer bottle or a crisp packet. Then, like the other local authorities, the council could not overlook the likely regenerative benefits it was becoming apparent that a restored canal could bring to the canalside communities. Crucially to the success of the canal's cause, Manchester city planner David Kaiserman appeared as one of the final witnesses before the Inquiry. He told the Inspector that Manchester City Council now intended to join the restoration partnership by becoming a member of the Rochdale Canal Trust, with the intention of ultimately restoring the canal to navigable condition through the city, reconnecting the canal to the national network with the Ashton Canal at Ducie Street and the Bridgewater Canal at Castlefield.

To the many supporters of restoration of the canal who had turned up day after day to listen to the evidence presented to the Inquiry, it was apparent that the Department of Transport's position was much less certain than it had at first seemed. The difficulties of restoring the Lancashire side of the canal were put in perspective by the work already carried out and planned on the Yorkshire side and by the W.S. Atkins' report, especially now that there was recognition in that report that significant benefits would be gained. The Department of Transport's line had always seemed remarkably short-sighted to the supporters of restoring the canal. They believed the highways engineers and civil servants had been blinded by a single-minded pursuit of building a road and the short-term Treasury-led precedence given to keeping the immediate costs down rather than considering what was best value. The Department had not appreciated the impetus building up to restore the canal, or how foolish it was to endanger that when already large amounts of public money had been spent on restoration. The door marked 'commonsense' had remained locked and bolted, unseen behind a fog of short-term economic thinking.

Michael Handford summed up the prodigious efforts put into the Inquiry by volunteers aided and abetted by the local authorities and their professional witnesses as: 'the longest, most expensive, most involved Public Inquiry ever mounted by the Inland Waterways Association during its forty-year history. For the small Rochdale Canal Society it has been a headache and a nightmare'. The Department of Transport at last accepted that the question of the canal was a major issue. There had been no new blockages created on the canal since 1974 and 'those who put in the blockages are now busily removing the blockages as fast as they can. The local authorities and canal society were on opposite sides of the fence... We are all on the same side now. Only the Department of Transport is out of step... They are delightfully antiquated as far as their views on canals are concerned'. During the course of the Inquiry the Department's witnesses had conceded that complete restoration of the canal might be a desirable aim, and – apart from quibbles over details in Atkins' proposals – that it was practical. All that remained was the question of whether the money could be found. He said that if asked 'is the money here today?... The straight answer is 'no', but with the political will and given time 'No, not today' was really 'probably tomorrow'.

With the Inquiry finished, the IWA and the Rochdale Canal Society began to count the cost. Between them, they had spent around £60,000 on W.S. Atkins' fees, together with more mundane items such as travel expenses, petrol for those who needed or deserved recompense, and astronomical postage and telephone costs keeping supporters and helpers informed. The IWA could no doubt write off this expenditure as part of the cost of defending the waterways but the Rochdale Canal Society had remained a small organisation that had no large reserves to fall back on. An appeal for funds was announced in the waterways magazines and the local press. Although falling far short of the cost of the Inquiry, a sufficient amount was raised to keep the society solvent, with Mr Arnold Ziff, the chairman of the Rochdale Canal Company, and its parent company, Town Centre Securities plc, making the first donation of £2,000.

Money was also at the forefront of matters being considered by Calderdale Council at this time. The council had failed in an attempt to obtain a government Urban Aid grant for work in Sowerby Bridge that would have included the canal. To make matters worse, central government was putting all local authority budgets under even more pressure than normal to keep costs down. The council was unable to find the money in its capital plan for restoration of the entire canal between the boundary with the Rochdale district and Sowerby Bridge before 1990, with restoration through Sowerby Bridge to the Calder & Hebble Navigation to follow that. All that the council could afford was to pay the extra costs over and above the money provided by the Manpower Services Commission to keep the MSC workforce employed, with hardly enough for the materials and plant required. A complicated financial jigsaw was approved. Spend a moment or two looking at this, and you get some idea of how the canal was restored and the determination displayed by Calderdale Council to find solutions.

The council had grant applications in the pipeline for funding help from the English Tourist Board and the European Regional Development Fund. It was hoped that these would help pay for the rebuilding of Longbottom Bridge that had been infilled as an access to Sagar Richards' mill between Sowerby Bridge and Luddenden Foot and the widening of the canal there where it had been infilled to allow only a 6ft wide channel; and for help towards the cost of the new bridge providing access to the Moderna industrial estate at Mytholmroyd, and for the new main road bridge at Copperas House, Walsden, that would be needed when work turned to the canal above Todmorden. Irrespective of the success or failure of these applications, £705,000 had been left to the Rochdale Canal Trust by the departing West Yorkshire County Council to pay for the new bridges at Fallingroyd and White Lee. Calderdale had succeeded in adding to this with an £80,000 grant from the English Tourist Board. This meant that, after spending on the Fallingroyd and White Lee bridges, the Canal Trust could release money to other schemes – £21,765 towards the new Moderna Bridge, £24,000 towards Longbottom Bridge and £31,235 towards rerouting a main sewer pipe that crossed the canal at Lock No.1 in Sowerby Bridge. But that was not enough to carry out these schemes. The Rochdale Canal Trust could borrow capital on the open market, and Calderdale Council could pay the interest on those loans from its revenue budget. The sums involved may seem large but they were trifling in the much larger picture of the Council's budget and transferring expenditure from its tightly controlled capital budget to the revenue budget neatly overcame the lack of flexibility in the capital budget. The Rochdale Canal Trust agreed to borrow to be able to contribute to the shortfalls; £24,765 for the Moderna Bridge, £31,235 for the Longbottom Bridge and £31,235 for the rerouting of the sewer pipe at Lock No.1. The Trust would also make a gift from the interest on the capital left by the West Yorkshire County Council of £6,775 towards the sewer pipe at Lock No.1 and £16,000 to the MSC scheme. This would help pay for rebuilding the canal at Sowerby Bridge from under the bridge at Tower Hill through the car park behind the main street shops back towards Tuel Lane.

This might seem tedious detail but within it lies a truth of major schemes. The imaginative use of whatever grant schemes exist and the ability to think out of the box in financial terms are essential attributes of successful waterway restorers and those restorers are in some cases just as likely to be found in the planning and

The new Fallingroyd Bridge taking shape. (Dick Booth)

economic development departments of local authorities as in the ranks of the
volunteer movement. While these complicated financial manoeuvres took place,
Dick Booth and the MSC team continued work. Not only did they build the new
Moderna Bridge but also plans were now well underway for Longbottom Bridge.
The Council had also approved expenditure on design work for the new channel
to be built in Sowerby Bridge, together with the demolition of the former Regent
Cinema that was needed to clear land for the channel and car parking to replace
that which would be displaced by the canal. The council was also planning for
work to start to the west of Todmorden, arranging for the Rochdale Canal Trust
to pay the design costs of the new bridge at Copperas House, Walsden.

Work on the new bridges at Fallingroyd, White Lee and the access to the
Moderna Estate, was complete by the autumn of 1986. On 21 November,
Councillor David Fox, the Mayor of Calderdale, and a party of VIPs including
representatives of the Canal Society and the IWA, boarded Calder Valley Cruisers'
trip boat *Sarah Siddons* at the new basin in Hebden Bridge to make the two-mile
trip down the canal to Mytholmroyd. Shire Cruisers' *Rochdale Pioneer* steered by
ex-County Councillor John Sully, another narrow boat and six small craft,
followed them. After descending Mayroyd Lock (No.8), they sailed through the
impressive new Fallingroyd Bridge, or tunnel as it was being called because of its
considerable length as the channel made an S-shaped curve under the main road.
The bridge had been constructed on the basis of a corrugated metal Armco tube
and the twisting route under the road certainly gave the impression of a tunnel.

The new bridge at White Lee, Mytholmroyd, near to completion. (Dick Booth)

The Armco metal tube structure of the new access road bridge to the Moderna industrial area in May 1986. (John and Margaret Fletcher)

Continuing through the recently restored Broadbottom Lock (Lock No.7), the boats then passed through the stone-faced concrete span of the new White Lee Bridge in Mytholmroyd and continued to the new Moderna Bridge where *Sarah Siddons* cut a tape across the canal. The official party stopped here but some of the accompanying boats continued to the stop planks put in by the MSC scheme at the Brearley Bridge. Work was continuing on the locks below as Dick Booth and his team worked their way back to Sowerby Bridge.

Rochdale Council was making progress through 1986 and 1987 on the route from Summit to Littleborough. Traffic was soon flowing on the main A58 road over the new Durn Bridge, which the former Greater Manchester County Council had provided £319,000 towards, and just above that, Durn Lock (No.47) would be completed in 1988. New gates were made for several of the locks including West Summit (No.37) and Longlees (No.36) which the Canal Society volunteers had restored by patching the old gates earlier. More extensive work was completed on Punchbowl Lock (No.40) and First Lock below Punchbowl (No.41) at Summit in the winter of 1987/88. Work on these locks was part of a contract for major engineering work where the factory of Fothergill & Harvey had encroached on the canal. A single-storey office block and the works car park had been removed from the infilled channel with alternative arrangements made within the factory site; the canal had been dug out again, with washwalls repaired

On the day before the official opening of Fallingroyd, White Lee and Moderna Bridges, Nigel Stevens and Dick Booth sailed Pennine Pioneer *down to the limit of navigation at Brearley Bridge, to check that all was ready. (Keith Noble)*

*The new Durn Bridge at Littleborough is complete, but there is very little water in the canal.
(John and Margaret Fletcher)*

and the locks repaired and re-gated. Rochdale Council also let a contract for recon-structing the swing bridge across the canal at Warland. The council received help on paying for this work because, in addition to the funds left by the county council, they succeeded with grant applications to the European Regional Development Fund for £12,869 for Durn Bridge, and £36,000 towards the running costs of their MSC scheme. The Canal Trust also received a further £73,000 negotiated by Rochdale officers towards reconstructing the canal channel through the Fothergill & Harvey site.

With about ten miles of canal available for cruising in Calderdale, the Council began the first of many annual payments from its leisure services budget towards the extra costs of maintenance of a navigable canal over and above the costs that the Rochdale Canal Company met to maintain the canal as no more than a water channel. Routed via the Canal Trust, these payments at first enabled the Canal Company to employ an extra two maintenance staff who would work to a schedule drawn up by Andrew Hardwick, the Canal Company's engineer. Very soon, the council would find it easier to carry out these works themselves in agreement with the Canal Company using the MSC staff from Callis Mill.

On Wednesday 30 September 1987, a small ceremony was held to mark the opening of Longbottom Bridge, where the MSC team had built a completely new road access bridge and dug out the canal channel to its full width, removing the infilling material that had narrowed the canal. Mrs D.J. Ainsworth of the MSC performed the opening ceremony and workers on the scheme were the first to sail under the new bridge. Paying for the work planned to extend the canal back to the Tuel Lane blockage at Sowerby Bridge and to restore Locks No.1 and No.2 there on the Calder & Hebble Navigation side of Tuel Lane was proving awkward, as the council's applications for European funding failed. However, the Yorkshire & Humberside Sports Council offered a grant of £90,000 towards Copperas House Bridge. That allowed the reallocation of funds by the Rochdale Canal Trust to start work in Sowerby Bridge once the cinema building had been demolished. A great deal of council officer time and reports to members were now concerned with how the council might pay for restoration of the canal through Tuel Lane and with possible sources of grants. As is frequently and frustratingly the case, parts of a financial jigsaw might be available, but only if other sources of funding came forward, and they proved remarkably unwilling or unable to help the council. Calderdale was not eligible for the European money that Rochdale obtained in Littleborough and at the Fothergill and Harvey site, as that was only available within the Mersey Basin area.

Meanwhile, the M60 Inquiry Inspector, Sir Michael Giddings, had written his report to the Secretaries of State to the Environment and Transport. He noted that: 'More than 900 letters were sent from all over the country... Some fifty Members of Parliament wrote to Ministers on behalf of their constituents [and] forty-four societies, companies, boards and others gave evidence'. He concluded that: 'incontestable benefits leading to a substantial number of new jobs would accrue

The culvert at the site of Longbottom Bridge before work started. The remains of the original arch are visible. (Dick Booth)

from a full restoration scheme'. The Department of Transport had approached the issue of the canal 'by and large in a negative way. Its witnesses viewed the [Canal] Society's proposals with all the enthusiasm of chartered accountants investigating the affairs of a bucket shop.'

(Wow!) The Department of Transport's witnesses had stressed the lack of financial commitment to restoration below Littleborough that was displayed by the Lancashire District Councils. They 'questioned whether Manchester City Council would grasp the nettle of clearing the shallowed section with public opinion divided, before Oldham MBC committed itself to clearing the obstacle at Failsworth. And why should Oldham MBC take the initiative when the City Council's intentions were so uncertain?' Sir Michael agreed that 'these arguments were never fully rebutted' but thought that:

> to expect [the councils] to have formulated plans for forward funding, against the harsh competition for resources in recent years and without any idea whether a further crippling blockade (i.e. the motorway) would be imposed at Chadderton could be described as naive. [He concluded that] while there is no certainty that through navigation would ever materialise, the continuation of the opportunity for this to be achieved is desirable for environmental, functional, historical, economic

The rebuilt Longbottom Bridge. The arch has been reconstructed and the roadway widened with an Armco culvert extension. (Dick Booth)

Restaurant boat Sir John Cockroft *at Lob Mill Lock (No.16) in July 1988. (David Evans)*

and social reasons. This opportunity depends on the proposed [M60] blockage being withdrawn. The cost involved... is not small but its expenditure would, in my view, be fully justified in the public interest for the positive and imaginative contribution it would make towards restoring and reactivating such an important part of the region's industrial heritage, and towards the economy along the whole canal corridor.

Michael Handford received a letter dated 10 March 1988 from the Departments of the Environment and Transport saying that:

The Secretaries of State have noted the very strong view of the Inspector that the canal should not be blocked by the new road. They accept that such a major blockage would effectively put an end to hopes of through navigation... During the Inquiry an alternative alignment in this area was put forward by J.W. Lees and Co. [to save the 'Boat & Horses' public house]. This alternative... could incorporate a navigable diversion of the canal within land which could be statutorily acquired by the Secretary of State... [The] Secretaries of State accept the Inspector's recommendation... that the Department of Transport's works should incorporate a navigable channel for the Rochdale Canal.

Michael Handford, the Canal Society and the IWA had won. The Rt Hon Paul Channon MP, the Secretary of State for Transport, publicly announced that the motorway was to be built in a press briefing attended by the chairman and secretary of the Canal Society at the Oldham Civic Centre on Friday 11 March 1988. The Secretary of State's statement about the canal crossing was short and – to the ears of David Marsland and Brian Holden – sweet:

> A question of great local concern was whether we should provide a navigable crossing over the Rochdale Canal. The Inspector recommended a change to the route to save the 'Boat & Horses' public house, which could include a navigable diversion. Indeed, I had a brief look at the area concerned on my way here today. We have accepted this recommendation. I believe that this will allow the local authorities and voluntary sector to make further progress with their plans for restoring navigation south of Rochdale.

The Canal Society newsletter mused that it was a sobering thought that 'the whole ghastly ten-year long business' was over a canal blockage that only existed 'on paper'; now thoughts would have to turn to how restoration could progress through the many existing and formidable blockages that actually existed on the route of the canal.

eight

THE BIGGEST ASPIDISTRA
IN THE WORLD

With the motorway threat removed, the newly extended Canal Trust – now a partnership between Manchester, Oldham, Rochdale and Calderdale Councils, the Canal Company and the IWA – produced *The Rochdale Canal – the Way Forward*, a document to press the case for full restoration of the canal. Reading this fifteen years after it was written, at first I could not think who it was aimed at. It was not worded as a document to help increase public support for restoration of the canal and there was no detail to support applications for grants. The trust was simply making a point that it, and the constituent local authorities, were serious in their intention of restoring the canal, and would need grants from central government or European sources to achieve that.

At one of the first meetings of the enlarged Canal Trust on 19 January 1988, Andrew Swaby, a planner with Rochdale Council, reported on the possibilities of receiving European Regional Development Fund grants that were then available for work in the Mersey Basin area. These might pay up to 50 per cent of the cost of work. The possibility of these grants being obtained for work in Calderdale, particularly for the Tuel Lane obstruction, was also being investigated. Although miles from the Mersey Basin, restoring navigation to the main network at Tuel Lane would have a beneficial effect on the Lancashire side of the canal.

The trust also considered one of numerous reports on water supplies to the canal. The North West Water Authority, as the successor body to the old local authority water supply departments, was bound by the legal agreement made when the canal reservoirs had been sold to supply a certain amount of water to the canal; that was thought likely to prove inadequate when the canal was ultimately fully restored. It was possible that the North West Water Authority could decide that one of these reservoirs, Warland, was surplus to its requirements, and for a period of several years, desultory negotiations continued between Calderdale and Rochdale Council officers and the Water Authority. At one meeting, it was decided to ask the Water Authority to allow investigations into the possibility of

Warland Lower Lock (No.34) was restored during 1987. (Adrian Rose)

MSC workers being able to carry out remedial works that would be needed both to the reservoir and to the canal feeder channel. A third report, written by Alan Taylor of the Calderdale planning department, who was responsible for actual work on the canal for many years, brought the trust up to date on Calderdale Council's plans for a new bridge at Copperas House, Walsden. Site investigations had revealed that more complex foundations than originally intended would be required and the cost of digging up gas, electricity, telephone, water and sewer services and replacing them in the new bridge would be more than had been thought; then contract costs were increasing generally. It was now thought that the bridge would cost nearly £300,000 compared to the original estimate of £190,000. By agreement with the Yorkshire & Humberside Sports Council, who offered to help restoration of the canal by a grant of £90,000 spread over the years 1987–80 to 1989–90, the shortfall in the council's budget was reduced to about £60,000 and the council hoped that this might be met by a grant from the English Tourist Board.

The highway engineers department in Calderdale was busy preparing the design for the work needed to extend the canal back through Sowerby Bridge to the blockage at Tuel Lane ready for work to be carried out by the MSC scheme. Looking at the council's files from this time, it is apparent that there was hardly any grant regime that had not been considered as a means of helping to pay for the major work of building a new channel back to the Calder & Hebble Navigation. A further £60,000 was obtained as a grant to the general MSC work from the government-sponsored Pennine Rural Development Area Programme but money for Tuel Lane itself was elusive. To ensure that the council or the Canal Trust was ready to act quickly if any opportunity for external funding appeared, design work was pressed on with to include the new tunnel needed under Tuel Lane and Wharf Street. Since the demise of the Metropolitan county councils, the highways and engineering functions of the former counties had passed to the district councils, but in West Yorkshire, for reasons that escaped me then and still escape me now, it was decided to retain a small central team based in Leeds to tackle major issues under contract to district councils. Calderdale Council now employed Keith Noble, who had helped the Rochdale Canal Society with engineering advice in the early years, in a senior capacity. It fell to him to organise and supervise this team, known as HETS (Highway Engineering Technical Services) when they were contracted by Calderdale to design and eventually supervise the construction of the new works at Tuel Lane. It was hoped that, if a 50 per cent grant could be obtained for the work, the Canal Trust would be able to borrow the other half of the cost. This principle of the trust borrowing to find the capital cost of works and the council then paying the debt over a period of years from its revenue budge, was extended also to Rochdale Council when the cost of the proposed new bridge at Warland was found to be more than expected. The trust offered to find an extra £50,000.

There was no shortage of enthusiasm in Calderdale for restoration of the canal, and work on the ground by the MSC team continued. By the time the decision on the M60 motorway was made, Dick Booth was able to report that in the financial year 1987/88 Sands Lock, Bottomley Lock and Warland Lower Lock (Lock Nos 32-34), between Walsden and Warland, had been restored to navigable condition. Lock No.34 was one of the few that required a significant amount of rebuilding, a testimony to the quality of the original construction. In addition to this work near the summit level which included dredging the channel and repairs to the canal washwalls and the towpath, work had continued in Sowerby Bridge on Lock No.1 and on dredging the channel and repairing the washwall as the canal approached the blockage in the centre of the town. The workshop at Callis Mill had been very busy, not just on work for the Rochdale Canal, but also making lock gates for Frankton Locks on the Montgomery Canal, Crofton and Caen Hill Locks on the Kennet & Avon Canal and Linton Lock on the river Ouse, and with work for other Calderdale Council departments making fencing and park benches. This brought in additional income to plough back into the scheme.

But the future of the MSC team at Callis Mill and the Rochdale Council team working on the canal above Littleborough was uncertain beyond the summer of 1988. The government replaced the Job Creation scheme with a new scheme, Employment Training. This was intended to do rather more than create temporary work by addressing the skills shortages of the long-term unemployed. The emphasis of the new scheme was to be on providing training rather than providing work. The unemployed seeking training would be trainees rather than employees

John Sully and the Mayor hammer a nail into the one hundreth lock gate to be built at Callis Mill. (Dick Booth)

and a training agency would send them out to be trained by training managers. If the Training Commission, which replaced the Manpower Services Commission, appointed the councils as training agencies and the work of the MSC teams was considered suitable for the teams to be appointed as training managers, then at first it seemed things might carry on as before. However, I know a little of the problems this new scheme caused for work on canal restoration. I was involved through the Huddersfield Canal Society that managed a scheme restoring the Huddersfield Narrow Canal in the Tameside and Oldham districts. The society was accepted as a training manager but had to take on a large number of trainees who had to be provided with off-site training in a special workshop set up for that purpose and at a local college of education and had to broaden the scheme to include training in office administration and computing. Had anyone known how the new scheme would pan out at the beginning they would not have even thought of using it for canal restoration; the Huddersfield Canal Society soon discovered the high costs of the limited amount of work that could be carried out under the guise of training and found alternative ways to keep their staff employed.

On the Rochdale Canal, as employees left the schemes on the expiry of their twelve-month contracts, the numbers available for work on the canal rapidly declined. In Calderdale, the council was not accepted as a training agency, and work at Callis Mill would therefore require trainees to be provided from the private sector training companies that had been appointed. A shortfall in numbers compared to the number of employees of the Job Creation scheme was inevitable and the new scheme provided no money towards the cost of materials. All the expenses had to be met from the costs allowed per trainee or from the trainer's own resources. The local press reported on the plight of the scheme and carried an appeal for sponsorship towards lock gates.

To help publicise the work, an opening ceremony was held when Lock No.1 was completed at Sowerby Bridge on 19 May 1988. The Deputy Mayor Councillor Mohammed Najib declared the lock open and named it the Albert Wood Lock, after the last major carrier on the canal. Albert Wood's son, Reginald Wood, aged eighty-five, was a guest of honour as Shire Cruisers' *Surrey* and *Sussex* carried guests from the council, the Rochdale Canal Trust and funding agencies such as the English Tourist Board and the Sports Council, through the lock.

Calderdale Council counted the cost of the training scheme and decided that by judicious juggling of their budget, income from the money invested by the Rochdale Canal Trust and income from external work by the Callis Mill workshop, Dick Booth's team could continue with a staff of around ten or eleven who would be paid as full-time employees. Dick Booth himself had originally been seconded as project engineer from the county council and on the demise of the county council from HETS; he would remain, but on a part-time basis and employed by Calderdale Council itself. It was hoped that up to thirty-five trainees could be attracted from the private sector training agencies. Rochdale Council faced a similar dilemma of how to continue work between Littleborough and the Calderdale boundary. Somehow, the work had to continue into the new training regime but the council was to find the recruitment of people with the appropriate skills almost impossible and eventually transferred lock gate production and fitting to the Callis Mill team on a contract basis. A ten-year programme to restore the entire canal through the district was agreed to in principle by the council's Environment and Employment Committee in June 1988. In theory, this was a big leap forward, but the Council could only make progress south of Littleborough if at least half of the costs were met by grants, such as the European Regional Development Fund grant. Rochdale Council did show a willingness to continue by letting a contract for the new bridge at Warland.

The Canal Company noted in the autumn of 1988 that all work on the canal had stopped except for the much-reduced workforce based at Callis Mill. The euphoria of the M60 decision faded rapidly as the implications of the change to training regimes and the need for massive grants on the Lancashire side sank in. But the Canal Society had not forgotten the euphoria. A wonderfully archaically worded invitation was sent out, saying:

> The Chairman of the Rochdale Canal Society requests the pleasure of the company of members and friends of the Rochdale Canal Society, witnesses who gave evidence at the 1986 Public Inquiry, representatives of the Inland Waterways Association, members of the Rochdale Canal Trust, officers of the Department of

Copperas House Bridge under construction. (Dick Booth)

Transport, representatives of the Rochdale Canal Company, Manpower Services Commission and volunteer workers on canal restoration, Councillors and officers of the Metropolitan Boroughs of Oldham, Rochdale, Calderdale and the City of Manchester and their Members of Parliament at a celebration dinner to be held in recognition of the decision to preserve continuous navigation on the Rochdale Canal through its intersection with the Proposed motorway at Chadderton. The celebration dinner is to be held at the Carlton Hotel, Hebden Bridge on Saturday 24 September 1988 at 7.30p.m. for 8.00p.m. and will be attended by the Public Inquiry Inspector, Air Marshall Sir Michael Giddings and other guests who took part in the Public Inquiry.

The celebrations might perhaps have been a little premature as the Department of Transport was soon to publish its detailed plans for the motorway crossing of the canal; astoundingly these showed a channel and bridge only wide enough for a narrow boat.

There had been no discussion of the size of the canal channel at the Public Inquiry. The Rochdale Canal was a broad canal built for broad-beam boats. Modern cruising and hire boats are mainly narrow boats built to be able to traverse the narrow canal network, so officers of the Department of Transport reasoned they could save a bob or two – or more precisely about half a million pounds – by building a canal under the motorway only suitable for these modern boats that were most likely to use the canal. All hell let loose! There were broad-beam craft

Craning the deck of Warland Swing Bridge into place, October 1989. (David Evans)

Beginning work to excavate the spoil and debris from the chamber of Hollins Lock (No.27), Walsden in 1989. (Dick Booth)

around, not just historic survivors, but new boats whose owners accepted a limited cruising range as the cost of more spacious accommodation. A narrow channel would prevent the operation of a broad-beam trip or restaurant boat that might otherwise happily cruise the Rochdale Canal.

There were changes in the Rochdale Canal Trust as it accommodated the additional membership of the Lancashire districts. Allen Brett, the Rochdale Councillor who had given evidence at the M60 Public Inquiry, took over from Calderdale Councillor Eric Whitehead as chairman, and the burden of administering the trust widened from just Calderdale Council officers, so it was Oldham planner John Billington who had to lead negotiations with the Department of Transport. Correspondence and meetings dragged on for the best part of a year, until June 1989 when officers of the Department of Transport and their consultant engineers met representatives of the local authorities, the Canal Trust and the Canal Society. Revised plans were put forward that showed a canal said to be suitable for broad-beam craft, but in fact, the canal was designed so that a full-length narrow boat or a broad-beam craft to short Calder & Hebble Navigation dimensions could just negotiate the bends. A full length Rochdale Canal sized broad-beam craft would be excluded and there was to be no towpath. Pity the poor boat horse, or the horse-drawn boat owner forced to pole the boat under the motorway! A diversionary route was to be provided for pedestrians via a bridge already proposed over the motorway. In the end, Dick Booth was able to suggest

Dredging the pound through Walsden between Lock Nos 27 and 28. (Dick Booth)

slight easing of the curves so that a full-length broad-beam boat could just navigate the canal if it was built exactly as planned but there was to be no towpath.

Meanwhile Calderdale Council was pressing ahead with plans for the new road bridge at Copperas House, Walsden (Copperas being a derivative of iron sulphate used in the dyeing processes of the textile industry), but the scheme was complicated by a financial squabble over VAT. Don't ask: you do not want to know! What this meant for the Copperas House Bridge was that the council would have to employ the contractor doing the work itself, thereby being denied the useful stratagem of the trust borrowing to pay the capital cost with the Council then paying interest from revenue over a period of years. Matters were not improved when the English Tourist Board turned down the council's application for a grant. The council bit the bullet and decided to go ahead, with work starting in January 1989. Whatever was spent at Copperas House meant that there was less available for work in Sowerby Bridge. The land required to rebuild the canal there back to the actual blockage of Tuel Lane had been obtained, the Regent Cinema had been demolished and replacement car parking provided ready for the Callis Mill team to build the new channel. With the Job Creation employees gone and hardly any of the new Employment Training trainees being keen to join the scheme, work was concentrated on the locks through Walsden above Copperas Bridge.

The cost of the proposals to actually build a new canal by means of a cut and cover tunnel under the roads at Sowerby Bridge was rising; the more trial holes that were dug at the site, the more problems were found with ground conditions and what had been buried under the roads when the canal was filled in. As work started at Copperas House, the cost of the Tuel Lane scheme shot up by a further £500,000. The idea of obtaining a European Regional Development Fund Grant from the allocation of that funding to the Lancashire authorities in the Mersey Basin area seemed dead in the water. The possibility of Rochdale Council submitting an application for a grant at Tuel Lane on behalf of Calderdale was investigated. The complexities of local government finance meant that any expenditure at Tuel Lane obtained in that way would be treated as though it was in Rochdale and count as part of Rochdale Council's capital expenditure; that was not something the council could accept when central government tightly controlled capital expenditure by local authorities. The Huddersfield Canal Society had set a precedent in obtaining a European grant towards an engineering study of Standedge Tunnel that crossed the border from the eligible Oldham district into the ineligible Kirklees district. Although for more than £100,000, the grant was much smaller than would be required at Sowerby Bridge and there was a significant difference between the tunnel continuing across the boundary and the Sowerby Bridge situation thirteen miles away from the boundary.

The issue of maintenance of the canal was becoming a source of concern, especially in Calderdale. The Rochdale Canal Company took a well-defined line; it was a private company with a legal liability to maintain the canal to a standard appropriate to a water channel and prevent flooding of adjoining land. The company was a subsidiary of Town Centre Securities plc and, therefore, indirectly responsible to the shareholders of that company. The Canal Company had property assets that provided a backbone of profit to the company, but its largest single holding was the canal itself and the management of that was the responsibility of the company. The company had long-standing relationships with the local authorities. It had seen their attitudes change from considering the canal as a nuisance best filled in where it affected road improvement schemes, to now considering it as an asset for the communities through which it passed. The company was willing (indeed was happy) to see the canal restored to a navigable condition but it had no duty to pay the extra costs involved in maintaining the canal in that condition – looking after the locks and paddle gear or keeping up with the dredging to a navigable depth. The company stressed that, unlike the nationalised waterways, it had carried out its legal duties without any recourse to the public purse. Waterway enthusiasts may have wished for more but the company was not a charity established for their benefit. To wish for more was unreasonable. Indeed restorers and potential restorers of derelict waterways within the nationalised system found that British Waterways was much more anxious to tie them down with legally binding maintenance agreements before allowing a shovel or a JCB anywhere near the waterway. So maintenance responsibilities were divided between the Canal Company carrying out the essential work to keep the canal as a watercourse and the local authorities taking responsibility for maintaining the canal to a navigable standard. In practice this was an issue for Calderdale only at this time because only in the Calder Valley was there any length of navigable canal in use by boaters. Options for future maintenance were considered: perhaps the Canal Trust could take over the ownership of the canal and the responsibilities for maintenance – but with the responsibilities came the liabilities too. Perhaps a way could be found of bringing British Waterways into the equation so that the canal could be maintained as though it was part of the nationalised network. No solution was immediately obvious and the arrangements between the local authorities and the Canal Company continued, but with the Callis Mill team carrying an increasing share of the work paid for from Calderdale Council's leisure services budget.

At the start of the 1990s, work on the canal slowed to a crawl. The Callis Mill team continued work but much more slowly than before now there was only the small full-time workforce and the occasional Employment Training trainee. They quite rightly were spending more time on maintenance of the restored section of canal than on further restoration now. Outside help was sought with a leaflet circulated to potential sponsors headed: '29 Locks restored; 4 locks to go! Money short!' The Rochdale Canal Society contributed £500. British Gas, British Telecom and Yorkshire Water contributed by reducing the cost of the service diversions required at Copperas House Bridge and local firms contributed: Warman International Ltd and Chas Openshaw Ltd from Todmorden, followed by contributions from national organisations – the National Westminster Bank, the

In one of several small ceremonies to gain publicity and sponsorship, schoolchildren watch the gates being lowered into place at Travis Mill Lock, Walsden (No.28). (Dick Booth)

Prior to the official opening of Copperas House Bridge in May, Dave Fielden had the honour of steering Grasshopper, *the first boat through the new bridge in March 1990. (David Evans)*

TSB, Marks & Spencer, who provided a set of lock gates, and £8,000 from the Halifax Building Society. Nigel Stevens of Shire Cruisers showed his company's appreciation of the work the Callis Mill team was doing by making a contribution at the time of the appeal and sending a second unsolicited cheque later. The Sowerby Bridge Rotary Club collected £1,500 towards the work in Sowerby Bridge. All of this was accompanied by small ceremonies to mark the help given. The Rotary Club's donation went towards work on Lock No.2 below the Tuel Lane blockage. The bottom gates were craned into position at the lock in a public event on 29 September 1989, watched by Rotary Club members and representatives of the council and the Canal Society. The chief executive of the Halifax Building Society unveiled a commemorative plaque to mark the completion of Smithy Holme Lock (Lock No.25) at Walsden on 6 April 1990.

The completion of this lock marked the end of restoration work on the western section of the canal in Calderdale. It almost coincided with the completion by Rochdale Council of the canal down to Littleborough, except that Durn Lock and Littleborough Bottom Lock (Lock Nos 47 and 48) still had no gates. Calderdale's Callis Mill team had built and fitted lock gates on the other locks between West Summit Lock (Lock No.37) and Benthouse Lock (Lock No.46). Also, there had been complications in completing Copperas House Bridge which delayed work on site and made the bridge considerably more expensive than anticipated with the discovery of rather more buried remains of the original canal bridge than had been suggested by the trial holes dug before work started. The total cost had risen to £460,000. With only the Sports Council grant of £60,000, that left Calderdale Council with a sizeable bill to pay.

The achievement of completing the canal to the county boundary was marked by a 'Crossing the Line' ceremony on 11 May 1990. The day started with Councillor Kneafsey, the Mayor of Calderdale, declaring the new Copperas House Bridge open, then over 100 guests saw him meet his opposite number from Rochdale at the county boundary. From the bows of two narrow boats nose-to-nose, they cut a tape across the canal accompanied by a canon salute fired by members of the American Civil War Society dressed in costumes (almost) appropriate to the time the canal was built. As always, maximum publicity was obtained with coverage on local television and radio as well as in the press. That publicity for the canal was continued with the National Small Boat Rally for trailed boats, organised by the IWA and the Rochdale Canal Society at Hebden Bridge over the weekend of 26/28 May. In addition to boats on the canal and public trips, brass bands, trade stands, Morris dancers and performances by Day Star Theatre

The opening of the canal across the county boundary allowed boats to travel down the canal towards Littleborough. An open day was held to mark the completion of the canal through the Punchbowl Locks and the Fothergill & Harvey site, where a small office building had been removed from the alignment of the canal. (Keith Noble)

In May 1990, the Inland Waterways Association's National Small Boat Rally held at Hebden Bridge provided an opportunity for these young canoeists to join in with larger trail boats and dinghies. (David Evans)

Company entertained visitors. There was a civic cruise for the VIPs and a parade of illuminated boats in the evening. Apart from spreading the word about the benefits of restoring the canal, the publicity helped put pressure on government departments to help to restore the canal, especially to find money for Tuel Lane. Calderdale Council saw the restoration of the canal as part of larger plans for the regeneration of Sowerby Bridge based on a restored canal and the repair and re-use of disused historic mills in the town centre. Encouraged by the political response from their approaches to government ministers, the council hoped that at last a solution to the funding of the new canal at Tuel Lane had been found in an application to the government's City Grant scheme.

The Callis Mill team began excavation of the new canal channel and boat turning area behind the town centre shops taking water back right up to the actual road blockage at Tuel Lane in the autumn of 1990. External work continued to be found for the workshop to help to pay for work on the canal including more lock gates but also level crossing gates for the East Lancashire Railway and engine shed doors for the Keighley & Worth Valley Railway. It was estimated that over £120,000 of external work had been found. At the Manchester end of the canal the Central Manchester Development Corporation had been set up by the government to take over certain powers from the local authority, with a remit to ensure the regeneration of a large part of central Manchester free of political control or the limitations of local government. With a short life of only a few years, these corporations were seen by some as a means whereby a Conservative government could take control from Labour local authorities and by others as the salvation of the areas for which they were responsible. Irrespective of one's political views, the truth of the matter turned out to be that some development corporations were very successful and beneficial to the communities they served and others less so. Insofar as the canal was concerned, the development corporation proved more able to spend money than the City Council had been. A quarter of

In the autumn of 1990, the Callis Mill team began excavation and rebuilding of the filled in canal channel behind the town centre shops in Sowerby Bridge. The stop planks under Tower Hill Bridge mark the connection of the new work to the original channel beyond. The new canal wash wall defines the shape of a winding hole (or turning space). The concrete pipes that took the water while the canal was infilled are being removed. (Dick Booth)

a million pounds was spent to dredge the canal, repair the banks and walls and stop leaks along the Rochdale Nine section of the canal. With the help of private sector property developers, Canal Street alongside the canal was transformed from a seedy thoroughfare to a thriving café/bar district and huge changes were taking place around Castlefield Basin with a new and rather glamorous footbridge, and a hotel and warehouses converted to loft apartments.

This was just glitz on the surface insofar as restoration of the canal was concerned. Nothing could hide the fact that on the Lancashire side, except for the intention that the Callis Mill team would fit the missing lock gates to the Littleborough locks, there was no sign of any progress at all although Oldham Council had lit the towpath through Failsworth as an important linear footpath and erected a series of totem pole-like structures as public art celebrating the importance of the waterway. The Central Manchester Development Corporation, the four local authorities and the Canal Company decided to seek further help from consultants that might be used to seek the grants that were essential and yet seemed so elusive towards restoring the canal. A consortium of ECOTEC Research & Consulting Ltd and Parkman Consulting Engineers was appointed to produce a £20,000 technical report to update the work that W.S. Atkins had carried out at the time of the M60 Public Inquiry.

The consultants reported that they had been able to review the cost estimates produced earlier. In most cases, detailed site investigation and design work was lacking but they believed that works in the Rochdale district would cost around £5.8m, in Oldham about £2.7m and in Manchester City about £2.9m. The latest estimate for the Tuel Lane scheme in Calderdale had risen to £2.5m. The options for upgrading the water supply for a fully restored canal were dependent on the uncertain plans of North West Water plc, as the water company owning the former canal reservoirs had become, following the privatisation of the previously publicly owned water suppliers. Warland Reservoir still provided the most likely option, however, and upgrading that would cost a further £2m. The capital cost of completing restoration of the canal would therefore amount to around £15.9m.

ECOTEC had previously carried out a study of tourism in the Calderdale district and was aware of the significance of canal-related activities in drawing people to the area. There was less data about the Lancashire side of the canal and environmental issues to consider but the consultants were able to make conclusions about a restored canal's ability to generate income from boating and other activities that might loosely be described as tourist in nature. Since Atkins had carried out its study, the potential benefits of a restored canal to act as a catalyst for increased property values and a range of residential, commercial and other developments had become more apparent. Excluding any leisure uses, to avoid double counting with tourism, the consultants believed that development-related jobs would more than double the number likely to be created by tourism. Together with the jobs from construction and extra maintenance work on the canal, 1,028 jobs were likely to be created by restoration. Using established economic formula, the capital costs of restoration work and the revenue cost of operating the canal over a thirty-year period were compared to the financial values over this period of the benefits achieved through increased property values and the jobs created. The result – described as a net present value of £12.5m – comfortably exceeded the sort of economic criteria that would be accepted by the Treasury as a guide for public investment.

A statement was issued that 'the Rochdale Canal Trust Ltd, Central Manchester Development Corporation, the four local authorities, the Rochdale Canal Company and the Inland Waterways Association are convinced that full restoration can be achieved and bring major benefits to the area', although it was far from clear how the signatories intended to achieve this. The four local authorities all agreed that they would do all that they could to achieve the complete restoration of the canal for navigation from end-to-end by the bi-centenary of the canal's opening in 2004.

In March 1991, the Leader of Calderdale Council, Councillor David Helliwell, officially opened the extended canal into Sowerby Bridge that the Callis Mill team had now completed. The turning basin provided for boats up to 16.7m in length and for the first time allowed boats to come into the town, without the need for a lengthy, slow reversing manoeuvre. Only a matter of the distance across Tuel

The completed canal channel and winding hole is seen from Tower Hill Bridge, but the route was still obstructed by car parking and the junction of Tuel Lane and Wharf Street beyond. (Dick Booth)

At the other end of the Sowerby Bridge blockage, the channel was soon excavated back to the old road bridge, and a new stone-arched extension to the bridge built for the footway. (Dick Booth)

Lane and its junction with Wharf Street and the short length of canal through Lock No.2 now separated the navigable water of the canal from the national network. The Callis Mill team immediately set out to reduce that distance by digging out the banking to expose the original bridge arch to Wharf Street and rebuilding the canal channel from Lock No.2 right up to Wharf Street. This was complicated because the carriageway had been widened when the canal was filled in and the roadside footway was on the embanked area. The team built a new arched extension alongside the original bridge to provide for a new footway. The Council was still hoping for a government grant from the City Grant scheme to restore the canal through the road junction.

In July 1991, the Minister for Local Government within the Environment Ministry, David Trippier MP, visited Littleborough at the invitation of The Littleborough Action Group. The group's aim was to highlight the difference between the work completed in Calderdale and the slow progress in Rochdale. A representative of the group told *The Halifax Courier* that:

> In Calderdale thirteen miles of canal have been restored and there are trip boats, hire craft and private boats on the canal. However, Rochdale hasn't yet completed the restoration of the section from the county boundary to Littleborough, just two and a half miles. We wanted to show the Minister the situation, draw his attention to the delays and make a plea for more effort by our council.

In 1991, attention was drawn to the speed of reopening the canal in Calderdale, compared to the slow progress on restoring the canal from Summit down to Littleborough. Trip boat Gracie Fields *can be seen busily carrying passengers the previous year at Shop Lock (No.18), Todmorden. (David Evans)*

It was true that there had been no progress towards resolving the problem sites on the Lancashire side of the canal at the blocked road crossings, at Failsworth shopping centre, or at the shallowed section in Manchester since the abolition of the county councils. Rochdale Council had worked at a much slower pace on the canal than Calderdale had, but had the Job Creation schemes continued, the two councils would probably have met concurrently at the summit. With the change to a training regime, the council had to pay for work by the Callis Mill team to complete the locks between Littleborough and the summit level and that work would not be complete until 1992. Rochdale and Oldham Councils had not been able to build the momentum that Calderdale achieved with the longer lengths of relatively straightforward work in the Calder Valley. The removal of the threat posed by the M60 motorway had not proved the benefit expected in helping the councils to make progress; there were simply too many expensive obstructions to navigation with only limited lengths of easily restored canal in between. The advantages of removing the obstructions accrued only when all of them were removed. That made it very hard to find grants. Rochdale planner Andrew Swaby had told *The Surveyor* magazine in August 1990 that 'because of restrictions on

With lock gates fitted to all of the locks between Summit and Littleborough, boats were able to reach Littleborough in 1990, but Durn Lock & Littleborough Bottom Lock still needed gates. (David Evans)

In 1991, the Callis Mill team fixed lock gates at Durn Lock (No.47). Littleborough Bottom Lock (No.48), seen here, was not finally completed until 1998. (Dick Booth)

capital spending the money is not going to come from traditional sources'. He was right. Indeed, the search for grants to help overcome the problems on the Lancashire side of the canal had proved fruitless. The European Regional Development Fund that seemed so promising had provided only small grants; waterway restoration was considered within the tourism category and the total pot of money for that category was small. It did not help that there were no designs or accurate costings for any of the schemes, but the councils had no enthusiasm for speculation on the scale of the sizeable design fees that so many schemes required, solely based on grants that might be received. The situation in Calderdale was different: the council was finding high survey and design costs but the speculation there was only over one scheme at Tuel Lane. The hope of a solution to funding the new canal at Tuel Lane was dashed yet again however as the government turned down Calderdale Council's latest application for a grant under the City Grant scheme.

With very little work at all taking place on the canal, the only way out of this dilemma would be by means of a new grant regime; governments of whatever political persuasion regularly chop and change the grants they make available according to the perceived needs of the moment. In May 1991, a new set of rules for judging applications for Derelict Land Grants was announced. Originally intended to deal with the dereliction left behind by closed down industry and mines, but increasingly concentrated on restoration of sites that directly created jobs, these grants were to be extended to cover schemes that restored land for environmental improvement where that improvement would enhance an area for investment. With the benefit of the ECOTEC report, restoration of the canal might be an ideal candidate; a Derelict Land Grant paid for 100 per cent of the cost of grant-aided work. Restoration of the neighbouring Huddersfield Narrow Canal, although later in starting, was rapidly catching up with progress on the Rochdale Canal, and there were close links between the two restoration schemes. Both passed through the Oldham district where the same council officers and the same council members were involved, and Councillor Allen Brett, the chairman of the Rochdale Canal Trust, was a member of the Council of Management of the Huddersfield Canal Society. The ability to compare notes became a very significant advantage in dealing with applications for grants, especially at this time when it was soon apparent that different officers of the Department of the Environment had different interpretations of the extent that a Derelict Land Grant might legitimately be used to restore navigation. Both canals benefited from the Huddersfield Canal Society's ability to negotiate with government officers in London, as well as in the regional offices outside of the formal arrangements between local authorities and central government. By the end of the year, officers of the councils on both canals knew that applications even for major blockages such as Tuel Lane could meet the criteria set by the new rules, if the funding needed could be found within the Department of the Environment programmes of work in the Yorkshire & Humberside and North West Regional offices.

Derelict Land Grants in this form presented only a short window of opportunity to pay for works on the canal. The process of submitting applications and the various stages that had to be gone through before work could start were slow, and within three years, the rules changed again. In the spring of 1994, administration of the grant regime was taken from the Department of the Environment and transferred to a new quasi-independent body, English Partnerships. English Partnerships would become much more concerned with the regeneration benefits rather than simply with restoration of dereliction, and it was soon clear that the new organisation was unlikely to approve grants in an incremental way, except with prior agreement in principle to the whole programme. We will return to English Partnerships in the next chapter.

The Derelict Land Grant was the saviour of the Rochdale Canal restoration programme. There had been several key turning points when success seemed more assured but when a large government grant was given to reconnect the canal to the national network at Sowerby Bridge, complete success was surely only a matter of time. Yet there was cause for anxiety at first, as the big grants needed on the Lancashire side still seemed elusive. The grants were administered by the regional offices of the Department of the Environment based in Manchester and Leeds, and the larger grants given by the North West regional office for waterway restoration went to the Huddersfield Narrow Canal, where Tameside Council and the Canal

Dredging the summit pound was a major task involving the use of a temporary narrow gauge railway along the towpath to take spoil away from the site. (Dick Booth)

Society had already paid for survey and design work. Oldham Council received £600,000 towards the Broadway Business Park on the site of the demolished power station at Chadderton. A mile of the canal was dredged, however, and the towpath repaired, and a new bridge across the canal linked the two parts of the site. Rochdale Council received £800,000 for dredging works. Potentially lethal heavy metals that had apparently been tipped in the canal were removed from the summit pound to a licensed disposal point and the dredging work continued down through Littleborough. The Department of the Environment indicated that future grants might be available, particularly through Rochdale itself, which, at last, gave the council the confidence to begin site investigation work on the culverted bridge obstructions to navigation. Also, to the south of Rochdale town centre, the unpopular 1960s' Ashfield flats had been demolished to make way for the building of the new headquarters office of Co-operative Retail Services, including a land-scaped frontage to the canal.

The Yorkshire & Humberside office of the Department of the Environment gave £168,000 for dredging the canal below Todmorden, where the early Job Creation scheme had been unable to properly clear the cannel which was now silting up; £57,676 for pressure grouting four lock chambers to stop water leakage through the stonework that would wash out the material behind the walls and destabilise the walls if left unchecked; £22,400 to deal with leaks; and £15,478 for building by-washes at locks. The big grant, however, was for Tuel Lane. At last, the canal could be reconnected to the national waterway network after nearly ten years of searching for grants.

Apart from Tuel Lane, the work in Calderdale could be carried out by the Callis Mill team. The provision of by-washes to the locks was controversial and objections from some enthusiasts – though not from the Canal Society, the IWA, or from boaters – delayed work. For a canal to be effective there has to be a method of allowing water to flow easily from the upper levels to the lower levels by-passing the locks, otherwise boaters using water at the locks could find themselves aground waiting for water to come down from higher reaches of the canal. The normal system on most canals is the by-wash: a by-pass channel either at ground level or in an underground pipe around the lock chamber. Some of the locks on the Rochdale Canal have a different system, referred to as the air-hole system, which by-passed water via the culverts used to fill the lock from the pound above through the lock chamber, rather than around it. Both systems had advantages but the balance of advantage was determined as lying with by-washes, if only because they introduced no complications for modern-day boaters who inevitably had less experience and expertise than the working boatmen who would be familiar with the foibles of a particular canal. Eventually by-washes were provided at most locks, although the historical masonry of the air-holes remained in place but unused. The workshop at Callis Mill was busy, building lock gates for the Pocklington Canal, the river Ancholme and the Chesterfield Canal, with park benches, picnic tables and other items for schools, local authorities and the National Trust, bringing in an income of around £100,000 in 1992/93.

Before work started at Tuel Lane, members and officers of Calderdale Council, the Rochdale Canal Trust and the Rochdale Canal Society visited the Kennet & Avon Canal at Bath. Two locks on the flight of locks there had been replaced by one very deep lock when a new road bridge was built over the canal. The plans for the canal in Sowerby Bridge included a cut and cover tunnel curving under Wharf Street and Tuel Lane with a similar but even deeper lock directly above the tunnel that would replace Locks Nos 3 and 4. With a fall of 5.9m, the new lock would be the deepest on the canal system.

The design for the lock produced by HETS being less than 60ft in length would have allowed only for short Calder & Hebble length boats. It was argued that with the short locks below on the Calder & Hebble Navigation preventing full-length boats venturing further, and with Library Lock (Lock No.19) in Todmorden having been restored only to that length, the considerable extra cost of a longer lock would not be easy to justify. Meetings between council officers, the Rochdale Canal Society, the IWA, the Rochdale Boat Club, the Calder Navigation Society, and commercial boat operators led to further discussions with the Department of Environment. It was accepted that lengthening the lock in Todmorden was possible and that Sowerby Bridge Basin was the natural destination and turning point for full-length boats. The money would be found for a full-length lock but, to reduce wastage of water, two sets of bottom gates would be provided in the new lock chamber so that the full length of the lock would only be used when a full-length boat used the lock. Just before the council went out to tender to appoint a contractor, pressure came from boating interests apparently not present at the earlier consultations. They claimed that the deep lock was 'a highly eccentric solution to what is a fairly straightforward problem'; rather than build one deep lock, the council should build a pair of locks joined together in a staircase with the bottom gates of the top lock acting also as the top gates of the bottom lock. Less water would be used, and boaters (used to staircases elsewhere on the canal system) would be less daunted by that than the very deep lock. Probably true, but a staircase lock would cost more to build, would need deeper retaining walls to support the adjoining land and would require additional space. That was an issue as the site was already so tight that the lock gates on the town centre side of the lock would have to be opened and closed by a rack and pinion mechanism because there was insufficient space for traditional balance beams. Even worse, a change of plan would require an expensive redesign. The council and the Canal Trust decided to press ahead with the deep lock, encouraged by letters of support from the Canal Society and the Calder Navigation Society.

The council and the contractors, DCT Civil Engineering Ltd, arranged a ceremony to mark the start of work on 17 March 1994. John Thornton, the council's chief planning officer, praised the councillors, council officers and volunteers who had worked and lobbied so hard to reach this stage. The chairman of the council's Environment Committee, Councillor Anthony Mellor said 'I hope it will act as a spur to the other Rochdale Canal authorities, Rochdale, Oldham and Manchester, to complete their restoration'. Brian Holden was quoted as saying: 'Twenty years ago we made extravagant claims that a new canal would bring employment, financial benefits and immeasurable pleasure to local residents and visitors. Those claims are now proven in Calderdale'. By this time there were thirty boats licensed on the canal. Naturally these were mainly based on the Calderdale length, although Rochdale Canal Society member Michael Greenwood had been keeping interest in the canal alive on the west side of the canal since 1992. He operated *Ariel*, a twelve-passenger trip boat, built by another society member and future chairman Ron Tinker, on summer weekends and bank holidays from The Rose of Lancaster public house at Mills Hill over the river Irk aqueduct. Baltimore Boats in Todmorden had joined Shire Cruisers in hiring narrow boats on the canal.

The first task at Tuel Lane was to dig an enormous hole in which the lock would be built; more than 10,000 tons of material were excavated and taken away from the site before the reinforced concrete lock chamber could be built. Despite all of the detailed survey work over many years, there were unforeseen problems. A geological fault that had not been revealed from the trial holes caused ground movements which, despite shoring of the sides of the excavation, led to a small building at Bank Foundry on the hillside above the canal having to be demolished.

Large-scale engineering in Sowerby Bridge. The great depth of the new lock is not immediately apparent in this view showing the fitting of lock gates. (Dick Booth)

The deep lock nearing completion, as seen from the parapet of the new tunnel under Tuel Lane, with the channel extending beyond to the section rebuilt earlier. (Dick Booth)

A large crowd waited expectantly for speeches from the VIPs at the official ceremony to mark the opening of the new tunnel and deep lock, with Oliver *and* Sarah Siddons *anxious to break through the tape. (David Evans)*

Waylon, the first broad-beam craft to pass through the deep lock, enters the tunnel under Wharf Street and Tuel Lane, ready to take VIPs to a civic reception in Hebden Bridge on the opening day of the lock. (Dick Booth)

Work was delayed as the supporting structure was redesigned and the tenants of the building relocated but the grant would be increased to just over £3m to pay for what could not have been foreseen. Work progressed with the lock itself and the section of the cut and cover tunnel under Wharf Street completed first, to be joined together as traffic was rerouted around the excavation of the tunnel under Tuel Lane.

Waterway enthusiasts from all over the country descended on Sowerby Bridge on the weekend of 3–6 May 1996 for the official opening of the new lock and the tunnel that would see the canal reconnected to the main waterway network. The new canal was certainly dramatic, with a 100m-long curving tunnel connecting under the roads. Boaters emerged from the tunnel straight into the new deep lock, which had two sets of bottom gates at 22.5m and 17.5m, so as to be able to conserve water. The event, organised by Calderdale Council with help from the Friends of Sowerby Bridge and the Rochdale Canal Society, was a huge success. The guest list included the great and the good from all over the waterways movement as well as the leaders, mayors, chief executives, councillors and officers of all four local authorities: the chief executive of British Waterways, the various funding agencies, the Canal Company and Town Centre Securities plc, the IWA and the Canal Society. Jim Saunders from W.S. Atkins was invited, as were John

Sully and Philip Darnborough from the early days of restoration. VIPs were transported in a restored AEC Regent double-decker bus in the glorious bright orange, green and cream colours of the old Halifax Joint Committee bus fleet. Over one hundred boats were moored on the Calder & Hebble and fifteen on the Rochdale Canal. Accompanied by the bands of Ripponden and North Halifax high schools, speeches were made from the bows of Calder Valley Cruising's *Sarah Siddons* as the lock filled. Some of the guests travelled on board *Waylon* to a civic reception at Hebden Bridge marina. The council ordered sixty bottles of sparkling wine for the event! The weekend continued with a festival in Sowerby Bridge and around the basin with sporting events, not just the obligatory beer tent but a full-blown beer festival, vintage cars, a craft market and canal society and other stalls around the basin ending with a magnificent firework display. The pubs in Sowerby Bridge ran out of beer and even the Methodist church ran out of tea!

nine

I NEVER CRIED SO MUCH
IN ALL MY LIFE

A week or two after work started at Tuel Lane, the new urban regeneration agency, English Partnerships, took over the administration of Derelict Land Grants from the Department of the Environment. As the deadline for that changeover approached, the Department of the Environment advised the local authorities to submit a combined bid to English Partnerships, setting out all of the work required, the likely cost and a timetable for complete restoration. Engineers from all of the Lancashire districts began to look more seriously at the road bridges, the motorway crossings, Failsworth shopping centre and the shallowed section through Manchester and put their initial estimates of the costs involved to the various projects. With inflation and construction costs having risen considerably since the estimates made at the time of the M60 Inquiry, the total cost was now thought to be around £22m but that included the work at Tuel Lane that was then underway. The report, submitted as 'A Strategy for Completing Restoration', showed a programme of work extending over ten years to the bicentenary of the opening of the canal in 2004. In a foreword, Councillor Allen Brett, the chairman of the Rochdale Canal Trust, said:

> A decade of successful restoration work has already highlighted the importance of the Rochdale Canal as a vehicle for economic and environmental regeneration... This document contains the strategy for the second decade of restoration work... It is only through full restoration that the Rochdale Canal will attain its true potential as [a] regional and national asset... [We] hope to be given the opportunity to release this potential for the benefit of a very wide community.

English Partnerships was willing to continue grant-aiding work; indeed within a few weeks of the new organisation being formed, further grants were announced for work in Calderdale. The programme to provide by-washes at the locks was to be extended with further spends of £80,000 in each of the years 1994–95 to

Contractors erecting the steel frame that will support the guillotine lock gate at Library Lock, Todmorden (No.19). (David Evans)

1996–97, and – very importantly – a grant of £69,000 was offered for the council to extend Library Lock (Lock No.19) at Todmorden. This would enable full-length boats to use the lock and continue down to Sowerby Bridge. The lock had been restored using the intermediate gate recesses at the short Calder & Hebble length because the road bridge at the tail of the lock had been widened, leaving no space to fit traditional lock gates at the full length. A similar problem on the Huddersfield Narrow Canal at Slaithwaite was being resolved by fitting a vertically rising guillotine lock gate tight up to the road bridge. The engineering consultants for that scheme, Wilde & Partners, were appointed to design a guillotine gate and their experience proved very helpful: the gate at Todmorden suffered none of the teething troubles of the Slaithwaite gate.

Although English Partnerships was willing to continue with relatively small grants, it was soon clear that the full amount required to complete restoration of the canal, even over a ten year programme, was far more then the agency would be able to provide, especially as a similar sum was required to complete restoration of the Huddersfield Narrow Canal. With large amounts of public money already invested in both canals, English Partnerships was not showing any preference between the two canals. The history of funding work on the Rochdale Canal had been marked by lengthy delays as new sources of finance were investigated but now – just at the right time – there was a new source: the National Lottery. The Rochdale Canal Trust and the local authorities (and several other waterway schemes throughout the country) recognised that the lottery could be a very significant source of money. Millions would be raised by the sale of tickets every week to go to good causes. The money raised would be divided between various lottery boards to distribute in the form of grants. Of these, the Heritage Lottery Fund was the obvious source for restoration, except that it soon became clear that Heritage money would go towards conservation of existing structures rather than to new or replica structures. The new channels required under the M62 or at Failsworth shopping centre would not even fit into the category of replicas. There were also plans for a special funding board, the Millennium Commission, giving grants to projects of significance to communities to mark the Millennium as the twenty-first century began.

On 23 March 1995, the Rochdale Canal Trust decided to bid to the Millennium Commission and, if that failed, to look again at the Heritage Lottery Fund. After further discussions with English Partnerships and, knowing the costs set out in *A Strategy for Completing Restoration*, an application for grant was submitted to the Millennium Commission. After some revision of the costs, this meant that the canal would be completed with a grant from the Millennium Commission of £11.9 million and from English Partnerships £10.8 million, with the total costs set at £23,171,000 and the local authorities making up the difference. The bid document said that the restoration of the canal formed part of a wider co-ordinated approach to canal restoration that also included restoration of the Huddersfield Narrow Canal to create a Pennine Ring of cruising opportunities. The ECOTEC report was quoted in detail to justify the expenditure in terms of the economic and environmental benefits of restoration. The purposes of restoring the canal were explained. It would provide benefits not just to the immediate area but also to the whole region. It would restore a missing link between existing navigable waterways and provide Pennine Ring cruising opportunities. It would improve the image of the area and encourage economic regeneration, creating up to 1,000 jobs. It would boost the local tourism industry and attract new spending to the area and it would transform the environment and provide new recreational opportunities.

The challenge of restoring the canal was said to be 'as great as the original achievement, testing engineering skills to the full providing solutions to restore the canal'. Implementation of restoration would be the responsibility of the Rochdale Canal Trust, a registered charity and a company limited by guarantee, whose members included representatives of each local authority, the Canal Company and the IWA. Individual programmes of restoration would be the responsibility of each local authority acting for the trust. A long-term agreement would be negotiated between the Canal Trust and the Canal Company to guarantee public access to and use of the canal. Maintenance would be undertaken by the Canal Company in partnership with the local authorities who would pay the extra costs of maintenance needed for navigation.

On 30 October 1995, the Millennium Commission announced that they would make a grant to complete restoration of the canal; English Partnerships let it be known that they too would be likely to find their share of the funding required. Everyone was delighted: Audrey Smith, the national chairman of the IWA, praised the work of the local authorities and the Canal Society who had done so much to see the fulfilment of their dream. English Partnerships continued to show their goodwill to the canal by making further grants for work in Calderdale: £270,000 for bank stabilisation works, £72,000 for further dredging and £38,000 for the replacement of the original Job Creation scheme lock gates at Lock Nos 14, 15, 16 and 22 by new gates made, like those at Tuel Lane, from Ekki, a tropical hardwood. The Callis Mill team continued to work on maintenance so that during the winter of 1995/96 for instance, they installed safety ladders and stop plank grooves at Lock Nos 1 and 2, new head gates at Lock Nos 15 and 16, and new tail gates, safety ladders and stop plank groves at Lock Nos 14 and 22. The lock chambers of Lock Nos 1, 2, 16, 22, 31, 32 and 35 were also pressure grouted to prevent leaks into the stonework.

The impressive view obtained from a boat leaving the tunnel under Wharf Street and Tuel Lane, entering the deep lock. (David Evans)

Boating in Hebden Bridge. (Courtesy of British Waterways)

As required by the Millennium Commission, the Rochdale Canal Trust appointed a project director. Ronald Rees had been with the Central Manchester Development Corporation with experience of running projects and dealing with funding bodies. He was based in the Oldham Council offices and Oldham took on the role of lead authority. At first, his aim was to persuade the Millennium Commission and English Partnerships to release funding to pay for the expensive detailed engineering design work now required. Because of the large number of obstructions to navigation involved in restoring the canal between Rochdale and central Manchester, this cost had always been an obstacle to the local authorities. Meanwhile, the Tuel Lane Lock and tunnel were opened, as we have seen. During that first summer of 1996, around 350 boats entered the canal from the Calder & Hebble Navigation and by now, there were as many as sixty-two boats licensed on the canal. There was no apparent progress with negotiations on the grants until the following year, when the local authorities came to a joint view that they should release funds from their own budgets to get things moving. That led to the Millennium Commission and English Partnerships offering about £2½ m in advance of the main grants so that schemes could be readied to go out to tender, and to cover the costs of several pilot schemes for the other projects.

By this time, the Millennium Commission had also offered a grant to the Huddersfield Canal Society to complete restoration of the Huddersfield Narrow Canal. On that canal, it took the partnership of British Waterways, three local authorities and the Canal Society three very hard years to negotiate the details before the Millennium Commission and English Partnerships would release the grants. I was involved and I know the issues. Both funding bodies required a guarantee that restoration would be completed with no further call on their resources, irrespective of the actual costs. The Millennium Commission required a cast iron guarantee that the canal would be maintained as a public asset for a minimum of 125 years. English Partnerships spent months checking and rechecking the consultants' work on the benefits that restoration would bring so that they could be satisfied that the economic regenerative benefits justified public expenditure of many millions of pounds. Although the Rochdale Canal Trust had a head start in that the Millennium Commission had offered a grant for the Rochdale Canal fourteen months earlier than the grant offer for the Huddersfield Narrow Canal, the trust found it even harder to satisfy the requirements of the grant-aiding bodies.

Towards the end of 1997, the structure of the Canal Trust was changed, in an attempt to move towards the requirements of the Millennium Commission for there to be adequate proof of a secure and maintained canal. Manchester City Council was concerned that the requirements of the commission would commit the council for many years ahead and, while remaining committed to restoration, withdrew from the trust. The IWA similarly felt itself unable to make commitments on the timescale required to satisfy the Millennium Commission; so the trust was now limited in its membership to Calderdale, Rochdale and Oldham Councils and the Canal Company. It became apparent that the Millennium Commission could not be satisfied in its requirement for 125 years' maintenance by any possible agreement between the local authorities or the trust and the Canal Company: there was no guarantee that the company would exist for that length of time. Although the history of successive reorganisations of local government structures suggested that the local authorities themselves were unlikely to exist in their present form throughout this long period, their responsibilities would have to be met by some body or other. So the option that occupied many months of negotiations was for the Rochdale Canal Trust to acquire the canal. A figure of around £1m was suggested as being the likely amount that would be paid to purchase the canal: the Millennium Commission, English Partnerships and the local authorities themselves, would meet this jointly. The local authorities would then collectively agree to make an annual maintenance payment of around £550,000 to the trust, divided according to the number of miles of canal in each district. Although Manchester City was not willing to remain as a formal member of the Trust because of the long-term financial implication, the council was willing to enter into this agreement.

Work on the restoration of the canal had stopped with the completion of the Tuel Lane scheme, although further by-washes were approved to be paid for by

The Callis Mill team fitting a balance beam to new lock gates, Tannersfield Bottom Lock (No. 68). (Dick Booth)

English Partnerships on 7 March 1997, and the M60 motorway including the new canal channel was built at Chadderton during that year. The Department of Transport showed the same degree of competence that had marked its approach to the canal from the start. The new channel as built would not accommodate a broad-beam craft: it had to be altered, and that extra work took place in 2002. To be fair, it was only a minor error created when last minute changes to the detailed design created a tight kink at the bridge under the access road by the Boat and Horses public house but it would not be cheap to widen the canal later.

Oldham Council, having failed to reach agreement with United Norwest Co-operatives Ltd over the land required to be taken from their supermarket to build the new canal at Failsworth, made a Compulsory Purchase Order for the land, and a Public Inquiry into that was held in 1998.

Negotiations dragged on as the local authorities and the Canal Company and its parent company Town Centre Securities plc tried to square the circle. Project director Ronald Rees told *Waterways World* magazine that the restoration project was getting 'very close to the wall'. The company was not satisfied that the deal being offered by the local authorities for the trust to take over ownership of the canal was in the best interests of shareholders. As time went by, it became less than certain that the trust and the local authorities could actually deliver restoration of the canal under the conditions of the grants as offered. Ronald Rees, Oldham planner John Billington and Chris Flintoff, the parks and open spaces manager at Rochdale, met the Millennium Commission staff time and time again in increasingly desperate attempts to make progress. Oldham and Rochdale Councils tried to force the issue by going public. A press release in February 1998 said that leaders of the two councils were appealing to the government for help and to the Millennium Commission to extend the deadline for acceptance of the grant, which was in danger of being withdrawn in favour of the commission diverting the funds elsewhere. Councillor Allen Brett, the chairman of the trust and deputy leader of Rochdale Council, was quoted as saying 'we have been haggling over details for months and have bent over backwards to meet the deadline.' He said that the trust had:

> Gone right to the top, including an appeal to the company chairman but without success... We are asking the government to lift the restriction that means the Trust can't have the Lottery money unless it owns the canal. And we are appealing to the Millennium Commission to give us a chance to get things sorted out before it even thinks about giving money to another area.

MPs throughout the North were backing the Trust's bid to cut through what the press release described as 'the red tape tangling up the canal restoration deal.' There was a whole series of scares as it became clear that no effective progress was being made. Not only could the Millennium Commission pull out of the deal but also the English Partnerships money was far from secure. In yet another reorganisation of responsibilities, the new Labour government decided that the grant-giving side of English Partnerships should pass to new Regional Development Agencies. Councillors Allen Brett and Sid Jacobs (Oldham) spent ever-increasing amounts of time trying to resolve the issues and lobbying for support. Rochdale MP Lorna Fitzsimons met the National Heritage Secretary Chris Smith and everyone else she could find to appeal for the restoration scheme. The chief executives of Oldham and Rochdale Councils, Colin Smith and Frances Done, took an ever increasing interest and Adrian Montgomery, the assistant chief executive of Rochdale, was brought in to help Ronald Rees on an almost full-time basis. Despite all this effort, the regular Monday morning council officers' meetings to discuss progress became very sad affairs with little real progress to report, other than engineering details. The original costings on which the bids were based had been little more than 'back of an envelope' affairs, and it became clear that, allowing for such issues as the rerouting of services and for costs of land acquisition, the total cost would be considerably more than the grants applied for, with little chance of seeing any increase. This led to serious work to reduce the costs. In particular it was decided that the Manchester shallowed section would not be dug out to its full original width but only so that it was just wide enough for two narrow boats to pass. It was not the best solution for boaters, but it had two benefits: it was cheaper to remove and dispose of only part of the material filling the canal and the spoil

The realigned canal channel built alongside the M60 motorway at Chadderton. (John and Margaret Fletcher)

remaining would shore up the canal banks, thus saving a large expense in repairing the washwalls.

As 1999 progressed and the Millennium drew near with no sign of agreement, contractors were working frantically on the Huddersfield Narrow Canal to meet the deadline of 1 May 2001 set by the Millennium Commission for completion of restoration. There was some work on the Rochdale Canal, on a scale that would have been cause for celebration earlier but now seemed puny in relation to works on the Huddersfield Narrow, as Manchester City, Oldham and Rochdale Councils completed the pilot projects that the Millennium Commission and English Partnerships had agreed to fund. These were significant because for the first time restoration work extended into Manchester City where the first two locks on the abandoned length of the canal at Brownsfield and Ancoats Lane (Lock Nos 83 and 82) were restored and the canal channel was dredged and washwalls were repaired from the Ashton Canal junction up to the shallowed section. In Oldham, the material infilling the road bridge at Oldham Road, Failsworth, was dug out and the original bridge found to be in a satisfactory condition; the Tannersfield Locks (Lock Nos 66–68) were cleared of their concrete cascades and infill material and fitted with lock gates and paddle gear. Just below the Failsworth supermarket blockage the major water pipe bringing water into Manchester, the Haweswater Aqueduct that crossed the canal just above water level, was replaced by a pipe under the canal. In Rochdale, a new swing bridge was erected at Little Clegg, Smithy Bridge. With work on either side of the blockage of the Failsworth shopping centre, it no doubt seemed appropriate when the government confirmed Oldham Council's compulsory purchase order relating to the land required to take the canal through the site.

Nothing was easy in the restoration of this canal. The council had made the Compulsory Purchase Order to acquire the supermarket site in 1997. The Public Inquiry had been held in 1998 when the Council fielded heavyweight witnesses led by Les Coop, the director of planning. Even then, the decision in 1999 was only reached after a massive lobbying campaign to persuade the Deputy Prime Minister, John Prescott, of the faultlessness of the council's case. To acquire the land required a huge commitment by the council. Restoration of the canal was seen as a catalyst for redeveloping the centre for the public benefit but the cost of compensation over and above the costs allowed for in the canal restoration plans would run into several millions that would leave a massive hole in the council's capital budget. The plans were not likely to be popular locally until the benefits of redeveloping the site were actually seen – which would take some time after the canal was restored through the site. The inspector at the Public Inquiry had simply not been able to see the benefits, which was worse. He recommended that the compulsory purchase order should not be confirmed. The chance of restoring the canal was at risk and John Prescott's decision to confirm the order was announced only after a massive lobbying campaign by the council.

The new pedestrian swing bridge at Little Clegg. (David Evans)

The Millennium Commission had extended the deadline for completion of work on the canal to the end of 2001 but only if the English Partnerships grant was confirmed by 31 March 1999, after which date English Partnerships' grant-giving powers would transfer to the new Regional Development Agencies. The last day of March came and went with no decision. Lorna Fitzsimons, the Rochdale MP, raised the issue in Prime Minister's Question Time in the House of Commons. The Millennium Commission extended their deadline yet again. The Canal Society, the IWA and waterway interests all over the country were lobbying for the canal now. Richard Caborn MP, the Minister responsible for the Regional Development Agencies, and Lord Thomas of Macclesfield, the chairman of the North West Development Agency, were pressed to come up with the grants needed. The North West Development Agency announced that provided they could be satisfied that the Millennium Commission funds were secure, they would make a grant but it would be spread over five years. English Partnerships had been able to move money around between regions and that ability had allowed them to offer especially large grants in the North West at the times they were required. The Regional Development Agencies did not have that luxury. They had to work within their individual annual budgets. The Agency offered grants of £1.5 million in 1999–00, £0.5 million in 2000–01, £0.5 million in 2001–02, £4.15 million in 2002–03 and £4.15 million in 2003–04.

That left the Canal Trust and the local authorities in a quandary. The Millennium Commission grant was conditional on the completion of work by 31 December 2001. There was hope that deadline might slip a little, but not to 2004. The Regional Development Agency's timetable for funding, with the majority of the money not available until near the end of their five year period, meant that the only way that work could be carried out within the Millennium Commission deadline would be by short-term borrowing until the grants were received. We do not need to understand the complexities of local government finance but my interpretation of the situation (in a simplistic fashion) is that the large amount involved was more than the Rochdale Canal Trust could offer security on and more than the local authorities themselves could borrow. So despite all of their efforts they were effectively back to square one. And the Millennium Commission's concerns were no nearer to being resolved than they had been when the grant was offered in 1995. The commission would not grant aid the scheme as long as the canal remained in the control of the Rochdale Canal Company, as that prevented the commission having a cast iron guarantee that the canal would be maintained for 125 years. The combined efforts of the councils and the Canal Company, all still partners in the Canal Trust and all still aiming for complete restoration of the canal, could find no solution to the impasse that would allow the trust to buy the canal. Even if they could, the local authorities would not be able to bridge the funding gap between the two grant regimes.

Most of the inland waterways in Britain are administered by British Waterways or the Environment Agency (as the successor to the old Rivers Boards), but there are other waterway authorities, notably the Manchester Ship Canal and its subsidiary the Bridgewater Canal. These various waterway authorities meet together on a regular basis in the Association of Inland Navigation Authorities (AINA). Councillor Allen Brett and Ronald Rees were representing the Rochdale Canal Trust at a meeting of the association when an opportunity came up for them to ask David Fletcher, the chief executive of British Waterways, if he could suggest any way out of their dilemma. Only a few months' earlier, British Waterways had created The Waterways Trust as an independent charitable body to take over the waterways museums at Gloucester, Ellesmere Port and Stoke Bruerne. The role of the trust was expanding so that it could act as a go-between in finding funding that was not readily available to British Waterways or local authorities. In this role, it would act as a major enabler, finding additional support for another large Millennium Commission funded waterway scheme, the restoration of the Forth & Clyde and the Union Canals linking Glasgow and Edinburgh across the Scottish lowlands and in raising the money to restore the historic Anderton Boat Lift in Cheshire. British Waterways was becoming very enthusiastic about waterway restoration, recognising that the growth of the network not only had financial and image benefits but also significant historic, economic and environmental benefits. David Fletcher himself had become especially enthusiastic to drive the process of restoration forward, and the Rochdale Canal would fit very nicely alongside the Huddersfield Narrow Canal to create a Pennine Ring of canals in British Waterways' portfolio. It was only fairly recently that the government remit of British Waterways had been changed to allow the extension of its interests beyond the nationalised waterways. British Waterways also had rather different financial imperatives to the local authorities. As a nationalised company encouraged by the government to act in a commercial manner, it was much less tied down by legal limitations of its activities.

The Rochdale Canal Trust had always thought of the possibility that eventually a way might be found for operation of the canal to be handed over to British Waterways, as canal management was hardly the norm as an activity of local government. Having tried every other means possible to free itself from the impasse, the trust invited British Waterways to help them find a solution to their problems. British Waterways was able to negotiate directly with Town Centre Securities plc and make a commercial deal suiting both sides in a way not open to the local authorities. At British Waterways' Annual General Meeting on 21 July 1999, David Fletcher announced that agreement had been reached in principle between British Waterways, The Waterways Trust, the Rochdale Canal Trust and Town Centre Securities plc whereby The Waterways Trust would acquire the freehold ownership of the Rochdale Canal. The Waterways Trust would receive the grants for restoration offered by the Millennium Commission and the North West Development Agency. To overcome the difficulties of timing of these grants over a period extending to 2004, the trust would raise a loan against the security of the guaranteed grant payments to enable work to take place within a timescale agreed by the Millennium Commission. The Lancashire local authorities would pay the interest on the loan. The Waterways Trust would enter into a contract with British Waterways to undertake the restoration of the canal and subsequently to operate and maintain the canal. The local authorities (including Calderdale) would pay an agreed annual sum to cover the additional costs of maintaining the canal for navigation. A complex arrangement and one that neatly sidestepped all of the obstacles to meeting the requirements of the Millennium Commission by putting ownership into the hands of a public body with a fairly secure long-term future able to guarantee maintenance and public access and to meet the timetable of grants suggested by the North West Development Agency. It achieved the local authorities' objectives of complete restoration, guaranteed maintenance and public access, satisfied Town Centre Securities plc and certainly satisfied the Rochdale Canal Society and the IWA who were jubilant that at last they could feel genuinely confident that the canal would soon be open from end-to-end.

The announcement of a solution was not an immediate get out of jail card; as ever the devil was in the detail and several months went by before it was announced that an exchange of letters on 16 March 2000 between the Rochdale Canal Trust and The Waterways Trust had completed the details of the legal agreements involved. Almost five years had elapsed since the Canal Trust submitted their application to the Millennium Commission and four years since the opening of the lock at Tuel Lane, and for all that time the future of the canal had been in the balance; always so near and yet so far. There was plenty of time for tears.

ten

LOVE, LIFE AND LAUGHTER

The twenty-first century had begun. The Waterways Trust had acquired the Rochdale Canal Company. With ownership of the company came ownership of the canal. The rights, benefits and obligations of ownership and operation of the canal had been conferred on the Rochdale Canal Company by Act of Parliament and only by actually acquiring the company could those rights and responsibilities be taken over by The Waterways Trust. When restoration was complete, the canal would be operated and managed as part of the British Waterways network but legally the Rochdale Canal Company would still own it. The company would be a subsidiary of The Waterways Trust. Boaters would no longer have to pay for a licence from the Rochdale Canal Trust; boating on the canal would be included in the standard British Waterways licence. By the time the canal was open from end-to-end, there would be as many as 121 boaters paying licenses to the Canal Trust.

Sadly, there would be no role for Dick Booth and the staff at Callis Mill who had done so much to see the canal restored when the restoration work was complete, although they were busy making and fitting lock gates on the Lancashire locks right to the end of the works. After that, however, British Waterways would employ their own staff on the canal. The workshop at Callis Mill still remains and continues to manufacture park benches, picnic tables and other wooden and metal items for Calderdale Council and other customers and can still manufacture lock gates, timber bridges and so on for other canals.

British Waterways opened a new South Pennine Ring office at Castlefield in Manchester, headed by Tom Rowe, an engineer, as waterway manager under regional director, Derek Cochrane. They were rapidly gaining experience of managing large and complex contracts to tight deadlines on the Huddersfield Narrow Canal, ready for a May 2001 opening. Keith Paylor was appointed as Project Manager with Chris Wearne as senior project engineer. Although the local authority engineering departments had done much of the preparatory work on engineering details, the works as built would be designed partly by the local authorities (e.g. Ben Healey and Smithy Bridges), partly by British Waterways and partly by design and build contracts (notably at the A627(M) motorway roundabout).

The legal agreements needed between the local authorities, British Waterways, and The Waterways Trust were concluded on 28 July 2000. Roger Hanbury, chief executive of The Waterways Trust expressed his delight to 'have given the green light to the restoration and... the massive economic and environmental benefits for communities along the length of the canal'. Inevitably, costs had risen since the grants were applied for and the simplifications of work decided on to cut the costs could not bridge the gap. Manchester City, Oldham and Rochdale Councils had to find an additional £3m, largely from their own resources. Part of this had already been expended on the pilot projects, although Rochdale and Oldham had managed to obtain a little help from Landfill Tax and Transport Supplementary grants. The total available for British Waterways to complete the work was around £25.7m.

What needed to be done? In Littleborough at Ben Healey Bridge, the B6225 road to Hollingworth Lake and Milnrow crossed the canal at low level, with the water piped through. A mile further down the canal a similar obstruction was met on the road through Smithy Bridge from Hollingworth Lake; a railway level crossing close by complicated the issue here as the new road would have to be kept as low as possible to provide visibility of the crossing for approaching drivers. These new bridges would be of a simple reinforced concrete box culvert construction faced in stone. At Smithy Bridge, the road deck would be as thin as possible; the public utility services would be taken across the bridge under raised viewing platforms alongside the footways.

Around Rochdale, six bridges had to be replaced. Firgrove Bridge carried the main A663 Milnrow Road across the canal near a junction with Belfield lane. Canal water was carried through a large diameter pipe. The new bridge would be similar to Ben Healey Bridge but faced in brick. The minor Deepdale Bridge had been replaced at a low level over the canal and a new swing bridge was proposed. To the west of Wellith Lane Bridge, a length of the canal where it passed the Sealocrete works had been infilled so that only a shallow channel, too narrow even for a narrow boat, remained. A new channel would have to be dug out and concrete lined. At Dicken Green Bridge, carrying the minor Dicken Green Lane across the canal, the water was taken through five small concrete pipes. A simple concrete faced deck was proposed on brick abutments. All that could be seen at Hartley Lane was a grassed embankment across the canal, again with five, small concrete pipes for the water. A timber footbridge would suffice here. Next was the massive obstruction of the roads at the junction of the A627(M) link to the M62 motorway and the major roads around Rochdale at Edinburgh Way. A large traffic roundabout completely obliterated the canal, which reappeared for a short distance, only to be culverted again beneath Gorrels Way. Not only was it difficult to design a new scheme to cross the motorway terminal roundabout but levels might be tricky at Gorrels Way because of the need to maintain headroom both for boats on the canal and for vehicles as the road tunnelled under the A627(M) immediately adjacent to the canal.

The bridge over the canal where the A664 Manchester Road crossed the canal at Castleton was infilled with brickwork and the canal water piped. Vertical concrete piles would be driven alongside the canal and faced with brickwork to form the abutments to a concrete bridge deck. Only half a mile or so further south the canal appeared to end, with its route blocked completely by the M62 motorway with the carriageways only a few feet above canal level. The solution here was to divert the canal to follow a new course for about a quarter of a mile. The bottom lock of the three Bluepits Locks (Lock No.53) would be partly filled in to the depth of the canal above so that boats could sail straight through the structure, then a new channel would take a course to the east of the original line leading to and through an existing farm-access subway under the motorway. Because the motorway climbs, there was sufficient headroom at this point. The new channel would then swing round to the west and include a new Lock No.53 before rejoining the old course of the canal. A small lean-to farm building would have to be demolished as the new canal rounded the bend near Maden Fold Farm to the south of the motorway and arrangements made to provide new access to the farm.

At last, after these obstructions coming so close together, with nine substantial blockages in the 4 ½ miles between Firgrove Bridge and the M62, there was a relatively long length of unobstructed canal, except that the locks treated by the Rochdale Council Job Creation scheme were far from navigable. Lock chambers were silting up and vegetation (even small trees) was growing from the lock chamber walls. None of these locks had been restored to a navigable condition. Top lock gates had been fitted to most locks to retain a level of water in the pound above, but there were no bottom gates and paddle gear was missing. With no maintenance, the gates that had been fitted were in a poor condition. Eight lock chambers needed to be cleared of silt and vegetation with the masonry re-pointed and perhaps pressure grouted; new gates and paddle gear were needed.

After crossing the boundary into the Oldham district, the short stone-built aqueduct over the river Irk was in a good structural condition but the canal bed was no longer watertight and canal water seeped through the structure. Shortly after this, the B6189 Grimshaw Lane crossed the canal by a low-level concrete bridge with just enough headroom for ducks. An unusual design of vertically lifting bridge opened and closed by four hydraulic jacks was to be built here. In another 2½ miles, including passing under the new M60 motorway, Failsworth town centre was reached. Here the canal came to an abrupt end facing the 'Co-operative' superstore. No diversion was possible in this tightly built-up area, and Oldham Council was in the process of acquiring the land needed to rebuild the canal. The supermarket would be demolished and the new canal channel through the site would eventually form the centrepiece of a new district centre, including a health centre, a new supermarket, other shops and new housing, when the council concluded negotiations to put together the land and developers. No sooner was the canal over this major obstruction, than it was blocked yet again, this time by a low embankment carrying Ashton Road West across the canal with the water piped through. That was closely followed at Poplar Street by a concrete bridge so low that the ducks that could swim under the Grimshaw Street Bridge would be lucky to get under here. Simple brick-faced box concrete bridges were proposed at both Ashton Road West and Poplar Street.

As soon as the canal crossed the boundary into Manchester City, the shallowed section began, with the canal remaining shallow through Newton Heath and Miles Platting for more than two miles to Great Ancoats Street near to central Manchester. The hardcore fill would have to be removed and taken away to a tip, nineteen low-level footbridges across the canal had to be removed, thirteen locks in varying states of dereliction would have to be restored and three new footbridges built. The locks had been treated as part of the shallow water section in varying ways with a cascade at the tail of the lock. Some were partly demolished. The pound between Slaters' and Anthony Lock (Lock Nos 76 and 77) and Anthony Lock itself had been subject to mining subsidence and would need building up about 1½m in height.

Dredging of the canal was proposed between Ben Healey Bridge and the Manchester/Oldham boundary and minor repairs were planned for the Littleborough locks. At Slattocks, a culvert under the canal also needed repair. As we have seen, the water for the canal which came from the reservoirs now owned by a water company was barely adequate. The option to acquire Warland Reservoir had not worked out because North West Water plc had decided the reservoir was not for sale. Engineering consultant's, Binnie's, had studied water supply issues for the Canal Trust and a figure had been included in the bid for Millennium funding to improve water supplies to the summit of the canal by back-pumping water up the Littleborough locks from the Hollingworth Lake feeder. British Waterways was not convinced that this was the answer to whatever water supply issues might arise; they wanted experience of operating the canal before they considered what further water supply works were required. The money involved would also come in very useful if diverted to help pay for the actual restoration works, where inflation, even at the low levels of these years, inevitably had eaten away any safety net incorporated in the original costings and the savings from restoring only narrow channels through the Manchester shallowed section were, perhaps, not enough.

The importance of the canal as a wildlife haven had been known for years. Just as restoration on a big scale was about to start, English Nature announced its intention of designating the canal from Littleborough to Failsworth as a Site of Special Scientific Interest and, to further emphasise its importance as a Special Area of Conservation under European legislation. In particular, designation was intended to protect the rare Floating Water Plantain found in the canal, one of the rarest plants in Britain. Although waterway restorers today are well aware of the importance of protecting natural habitats, this meant that British Waterways had to take special care to ensure that the canal was restored not just for boaters, walkers and anglers, but also to the benefit of natural habitats, wildlife and plant species. Ecologist Jason Leach was brought in to ensure that this was recognised as work progressed and that particular care was taken to provide a number of offside areas reserved for wildlife from which boats were excluded.

Digging out the shallowed section at Grimshaw Lane between Newton Heath and Miles Platting, January 2002. (John and Margaret Fletcher)

On 10 November 2000, Environment Minister Michael Meacher launched the Millennium restoration works at Failsworth, appropriately in his own constituency, and by the spring of 2001, large-scale works were underway. Wrekin Construction, a company well used to working on waterways, was digging out the shallowed section, and Land & Water, a contract dredging company, was busy in the Rochdale area. British Waterways' own staff had fettled up the Littleborough flight of locks. Contracts had been awarded to A.E. Yates Ltd for the new bridges at Ben Healey and Smithy Bridges, and to the large contracting firm of Balfour Beatty for the £3.5m works on perhaps the most difficult job of all: restoring the canal through the Edinburgh Way and Gorrels Way blockages at the terminal round-about of the A627(M) in Rochdale. Working closely with British Waterways' engineers and the council's highways engineers, Balfour Beatty and their engineering consultants, Gifford's, evolved a new design here that would overcome the massive difficulties of raising road levels to allow the building of the canal through the junction while keeping heavy road traffic flowing. A long concrete box culvert tunnel would be built across the centre of the roundabout, then, by careful juggling of traffic flows and temporary diversions, the road junction would be completely remodelled so that traffic passed over the tunnel to a new traffic light-controlled junction. That suited the highways engineers as a lights controlled junction with separate slip roads to handle turning traffic could handle larger traffic flows than the original roundabout. When traffic was rerouted at the new higher level over

The formerly shallowed section seen from Varley Street, Miles Platting, with material remaining to support the banks of the canal, and only a narrow channel excavated. (John and Margaret Fletcher)

the box tunnel of the canal, the tunnel could be extended so that the slip roads could be built for turning traffic. And the level of the canal worked out just right to get a second bridge in here under Gorrels Way with enough headroom both for boats and for traffic passing along Gorrels Way under the A627(M). Work started on this complex task in July 2001.

By the end of 2001, traffic was being diverted or directed on temporary bridges or embankments at Ben Healey Bridge, Firgrove Bridge and Manchester Road Bridge, Castleton. The narrow channel being created with wider passing places on significant lengths of the shallowed section was causing concern to potential boaters on the canal but the truth was that this was all that could be afforded with the money available. By spring 2002, work had started at Dicken Green and Hartley Lane Bridges and on the refurbishment of the locks at Bluepits (Lock Nos 51–53), Slattocks (Lock Nos 54–59), Boarshaw (Lock No.60) and Scowcroft (Lock No.61). The 'Co-operative' supermarket at Failsworth had been demolished and the route of the canal cleared; work had started on the Ashton Road West and Poplar Street Bridges. In fact, work was now taking place at all of the obstructions on the canal. The Sealocrete diversion had started and also the central canal tunnel at the A627(M) road junction. Work was taking place on the locks in the shallowed section, some of which showed how tight the budget was by the use of concrete and artificial stone. The subsided channel between Lock Nos 76 and 77 and Anthony Lock itself (Lock No.77) were being raised in concrete.

Constructing the new concrete box section tunnel across the terminal roundabout of the A627(M), Rochdale. (Courtesy of Mike Poloway on behalf of British Waterways)

The same aerial view as the previous illustration with the route of the canal and the new road junction superimposed. (Courtesy of Mike Poloway on behalf of British Waterways)

The main road bridge nearing completion, Manchester Road, Castleton. (John amd Margaret Fletcher)

An aerial view showing the canal rebuilt through the site of the demolished 'Co-operative' super-market at Failsworth, with cleared land alongside awaiting redevelopment. (Courtesy of Mike Poloway on behalf of British Waterways)

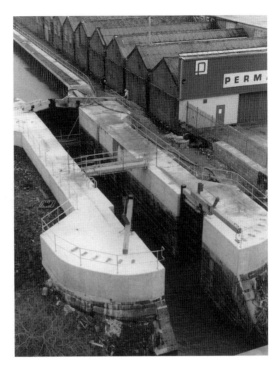

Anthony Lock (No.77) showing how the lock sides and the banks of the canal above the lock have been raised in concrete to counter mining subsidence. (Courtesy of Mike Poloway on behalf of British Waterways)

Ben Healey Bridge, Littleborough. (John and Margaret Fletcher)

Aerial view of the entire length of the M62 motorway diversion of the canal under construction. (Courtesy of Mike Poloway on behalf of British Waterways)

Building the new channel to the north of the motorway. (Courtesy of Mike Poloway on behalf of British Waterways)

Keith Paylor, British Waterways' project engineer, studies the plans at the new Lock No.53 to the south of the motorway. (Courtesy of Mike Poloway on behalf of British Waterways)

The canal under the M62 motorway, built through a former farm access subway. (David Evans)

Time was getting very short for completion by July when the new Ben Healey Bridge was opened in March, the culvert under Slattocks embankment was relined, the channel was dug out and the reinforced concrete channel was underway at Failsworth. Traffic was diverted over the new canal tunnel at the A627(M) junction and new lock gates were appearing on the Blue Pits and Slattocks locks. Over 100 wrecked cars and huge numbers of shopping trolleys had been taken out of the canal, even from the shallowed section.

Work had not started on the crucial M62 crossing. The landowners had appealed to the High Court over the government's approval of a compulsory purchase order to obtain the land. The appeal was not heard until May when the High Court found in favour of the canal, leaving just five weeks to build the new channel under the motorway and the new lock back down to the canal.

Only a week before the canal was due to open, work was going on at a frantic pace. Ashton Road and Poplar Street Bridges were unfinished; work was well on with building the new Lock No.53 at the M62 motorway crossing but, to the north of the motorway, the new channel was only just being defined by driving steel piles that would form the new banks between which the canal still had to be excavated. The massive Edinburgh Way/Gorrels Way work at the A627(M) junction was nearly complete, apart from a mass of traffic cones, temporary traffic lights and scaffolding that had to be removed from the site. There was no sign yet of the hydraulically operated lift bridge at Grimshaw Lane, where traffic remained diverted on a temporary bridge.

I was amazed that work on the Huddersfield Narrow Canal had been finished in time for the canal to reopen but that was nothing compared to this. This defied belief. Could it be done? The press were shown the works underway only a few days before the opening, and IWA North West Region chairman John Fletcher looked at the same time. He was convinced it was not possible. I was inclined to agree with him. We were wrong! On 1 July 2002 there was navigable water from Sowerby Bridge all the way to Ducie Street Junction. The Rochdale Canal was open from end-to-end again. Admittedly boaters had to exercise great care and put up with occasional delays as the contractors beavered away to complete the remaining works and tidy up the debris of construction but that was nothing compared to the feat of completing these complex works in such a short timescale, especially at the M62 where the main work had only started five weeks before the opening day.

After the multiple reopening ceremonies on the other Millennium Commission funded waterway restorations of the Forth & Clyde and Union Canals in Scotland and the nearby Huddersfield Narrow Canal, British Waterways announced that there would be 'celebrations to mark the completion of restoration works'. So in Manchester on the morning of 1 July, representatives of The Waterways Trust, British Waterways, Manchester City Council, the Rochdale Canal Trust, the Millennium Commission, the North West Development Agency and the Rochdale Canal Society met at Duke's Lock (Lock No.92) at the entrance

Broadcaster and vice-president of The Waterways Trust, John Craven cuts the ribbon to mark the completion of restoration works at Duke's Lock (No. 92), Castlefield, Manchester, 1 July 2002. Behind him, from left to right are: Derek Cochrane (regional director, British Waterways), Councillor Allen Brett (chairman, Rochdale Canal Trust), and Roger Hanbury (chief executive, The Waterways Trust). (David Evans)

Later the same day, steeplejack, amateur industrial archaeologist and television personality, Fred Dibnah cut the tape at Ben Healey Bridge, the northern end of the section of the canal in Lancashire restored under the Millennium project. (David Evans)

to the canal from Castlefield Basin. John Craven, broadcaster and vice-president of The Waterways Trust, cut a ribbon from the bows of Shire Cruisers' narrow boat *Worcester*.

Meanwhile, at Littleborough a large crowd, said by the Canal Society to number several thousand people, were entertained by a brass band sheltering from the pouring rain in a marquee. With just enough time for the Canal Society contingent to arrive from the Manchester ceremony, a flotilla of boats led by the historic horse-drawn boat *Elland* came down the canal to stop at Ben Healey Bridge. Steeplejack, amateur industrial archaeologist and television personality, Fred Dibnah, standing on the bows of *Elland*, nearly cut the tape across the canal several times in his speech as he thought of other things to say about a canal that had stood the test of time, before he finally cut the tape to declare the Lancashire section of the canal open.

Members of the local authorities, the Rochdale Canal Trust and the Rochdale Canal Society were jubilant. They had achieved their aim of seeing the canal restored to full navigation twenty-eight years after the formation of the Canal Society. David Fletcher, the Chief Executive of British Waterways rightly said that the restoration of the canal had been a triumph of working in partnership.

Boats began to use the entire canal. When the narrow boat *Katherine* arrived at Ducie Street Junction at 2.55p.m. on Wednesday 3 July, it was the first boat to pass along the entire length of the canal since the *May Queen* in 1939. Very appropriately, Shire Cruisers' *Westmoreland* was the first to complete a west to east crossing, reaching Sowerby Bridge on 6 July, closely followed by *Worcester* that had starred in the Manchester ceremony with John Craven. By the end of the year, 400 boats had been through the formerly shallowed section in Manchester, where (having learned from problems faced by boaters on the newly opened Huddersfield Narrow and Forth & Clyde Canals the previous year) British Waterways staff were escorting boats through in small convoys. There had been 800 boat movements across the summit level and, throughout the year, more than 2,000 boats through the deep lock at Tuel Lane. Some boaters had struggled on the newly opened length with heavy paddle gear and lock gates and variable quantities of water, and the canal was closed for several weeks in 2003 following the failure of several of the early Job Creation scheme lock gates, the result, perhaps, of the timbers having dried out, as unused locks remained empty for too long. Boaters and local waterway enthusiasts also have doubts that there will be sufficient water without

A jubilant Brian Holden, long-standing secretary of the Rochdale Canal Society, graced the cover of the issue of the society's newsletter after the reopening of the canal from end-to-end. (Rochdale Canal Society)

The formal opening ceremony at the A627(M) crossing in Rochdale, 28 March 2003. From left to right: Derek Cochrane (regional director, British Waterways), Lorna Fitzsimons, MP for Rochdale, and Michael Meacher MP are unveiling the plaques. (David Evans)

the Littleborough locks back-pumping scheme. These sorts of problems have afflicted all long-lasting waterway restorations and, as in other restored canals, they will be overcome with usage of the canal over time; they do not detract from the achievement of having reopened the canal to navigation.

That achievement was formally recognised on 28 March 2003 when the Environment Minister, Michael Meacher MP, officially opened the canal at the upstream end of the new A627(M) tunnel. He unveiled two plaques on a temporary wooden plinth that would be re-sited in the Oldham and Rochdale districts. Rochdale Canal Society chairman, Ron Tinker presented commemorative plates to Mr Meacher and the other speakers and a bouquet of flowers was presented to Councillor Lisl Murphy, the Mayor of Rochdale. The Minister concluded the event by planting a specimen of floating water plantain in the canal. The Rochdale Canal Society newsletter commented on the society's 'intense satisfaction' that the 'society's aim of restoring the canal as a through navigation had been achieved' and that it now remained for the canal's supporters 'to ensure the canal can succeed as Britain's highest broad waterway'.

I have not been able to establish precisely how much the restoration of the canal has cost; indeed, I doubt that the exercise is possible. The local authorities have not retained all of the early files and much of the early work was intended more for job creation and to create a pleasant linear space rather than for restoration of the canal to navigation. Then the high cost of acquisition of the land needed for the canal at Failsworth was spent to allow for the creation of a new centre there, as well as the restoration of the canal. For what it is worth my, very rough, estimate (excluding the M60 crossing) is around £45m, and possibly slightly more.

Was it all worth it? Environmentally, it was a triumph; the canal provides a magnificent central feature to the middle and upper Calder Valley and the upper Roch Valley and the communities between Rochdale and Manchester but the money was provided essentially for the economic and community benefits. Take a look at Hebden Bridge and you will be in no doubt that those will follow. Early indications are that, with a restored waterway, similar benefits will follow all along

The attraction of the restored canal. Boats at the Millennium Rally, Hebden Bridge, September 2000. (David Evans)

'The canals – aren't they fantastic… let's create a new Amsterdam, a new East Manchesterdam, a special place in the city' (Tom Bloxham MBE, chairman, Urban Splash). This is the architect's drawing of the New Islington development, showing the historic Ancoats Mills, the Rochdale Canal and a new canal to be built as part of the development curving away to the right that will connect to the Ashton Canal. (Courtesy of Urban Splash/Alsop Architects)

the urban parts of the canal, which will far outweigh the cost and disruption of the work of restoration. Already new waterway links are planned in Manchester, reopening disused and filled in arms of the canal as central features of the plans for replacing the 1960s' Cardroom housing estate with the new and, hopefully, architecturally exciting New Islington development. Alongside the canal four buildings of the now disused but historically important Royal Mills complex in Ancoats are to be converted to apartments, a business centre, shops and restaurants, building on the working locks and moving boats of the attractive waterside environment provided by the canal. At the other end of the canal, plans for the remaining disused warehouses in the basin at Sowerby Bridge have finally come to fruition. These sites all have the opportunity of being developments of a high architectural and environmental standard, rather than the sadly too common developers' pastiche, pretending to be in the style of a previous age but having no sense of place or respect for their environment. Other developments will follow in Fairfield, Rochdale and Littleborough, capitalising on the waterside environment; some we will no doubt regret, but if even half of them meet a decent standard of design and respect for a sense of place, then the canal corridor will be a far better place. Oldham and Rochdale Councils have adopted a canal corridor strategy to plan for bringing this new life to the area.

If the late Dr Cyril Boucher could walk the towpath again, he would be astounded that the canal, which was in such a sorry state when he made his annual

walks along it, is again open to navigation. Even better, in years to come the waterside will be bordered by living thriving communities rather than the increasing dereliction and desolation that Dr Boucher saw in the 1950s and 1960s. It truly is astounding that so much change can come from one simple idea – that the canal could be brought back to life – and that all of this should have developed from the ideas of a few people who the rest of the world thought were well-meaning, but misguided cranks.

Beautiful Calder Valley scenery at Shade Lock (No.21), with Gauxholme Locks beyond the castellated railway bridge. (Courtesy of British Waterways)

APPENDIX

RESTORING THE CANAL

The obstructions to navigation and notes on who carried out restoration work.

NOTES:

(i) The canal pounds between the locks are not listed unless infilled. Those that remained in water were generally restored together with adjacent locks, apart from the summit pound and a length in Chadderton that are mentioned separately.

(ii) The dates given are those for the completion of work. In the case of locks in the Rochdale and Oldham districts restored by job creation labour, these are in some cases several years after work on clearing the lock chambers because the locks cannot be considered to have been restored until lock gates and paddle gear were fitted.

(iii) Callis refers to work carried out by Calderdale Council's team at Callis Mill, at first using job creation labour, but after 1988 with full-time employees.

(iv) MSC refers to other job creation work by Rochdale and Oldham Councils.

(v) MP refers to work carried out by the partnership of the Lancashire local authorities and British Waterways paid for largely by the Millennium Commission and the North West Development Agency.

Concrete weir blocking access to the canal from Sowerby Bridge Basin	Calderdale MBC	1974
Albert Wood Lock (No.1)	Callis	1988
Second Sowerby Bridge Lock (No.2)	Callis	1990
Wharf Street/Tuel Lane junction (canal culverted) and car park on infilled channel to Tower Hill Bridge, Sowerby Bridge. Lock Nos 3 and 4 buried.		
	(a) Re-excavation of channel from Tower Hill to Tuel Lane – Callis	1991
	(b) Re-excavation of channel from Lock No.2 to Wharf Street and extension to Wharf Street Bridge – Callis	1992
	(c) Tuel Lane deep lock replacing Lock Nos 3 and 4 and tunnel under Tuel Lane/Wharf Street – Calderdale MBC	1996
Sagar Richards narrowed section	Callis	1987
Longbottom Bridge	New bridge - Callis	1987
Brearley Lower or Edward Kilner Lock (No.5)	Callis	1987
Brearley Lock (No.6)	Callis	1986
Moderna Bridge	New bridge – Callis/Calderdale MBC	1986
White Lee Bridge	New bridge – Calderdale MBC	1986
Broadbottom Lock (No.7)	Callis	1984
Fallingroyd Bridge	New bridge – Calderdale MBC	1986

Mayroyd Lock (No.8)	Callis	1984
Blackpit Lock (No.9)	Callis	1984
Hebble End Bridge	New bridge – West Yorkshire C.C.	1983
Stubbing Lower Lock (No.10)	Callis	1984
Stubbing Upper Lock (No.11)	Callis	1984
Rawden Mill Lock (No.12)	Callis	1983
Callis Lock (No.13)	Callis	1983
Holmcoat Lock (No.14)	Callis	1983
Shawplains Lock (No.15)	Callis	1983
Lob Mill Lock (No.16)	Callis	1983
Old Royd Lock (No.17)	Callis	1983
Shop Lock (No.18)	Callis	1983
Library or Todmorden Lock (No.19)	Callis (restored as short lock)	1982
	Extended with guillotine gate – Calderdale MBC	1995
Wadsworth Mill Lock (No.20)	Callis	1985
Shade Lock (No.21)	Callis	1985
Gauxholme Lowest Lock (No.22)	Callis	1984
Gauxholme Middle Lock (No.23)	Callis	1985
Gauxholme Highest Lock (No.24)	Callis	1984
Copperas House Bridge	New bridge – Calderdale MBC	1990
Smithyholme Lock (No.25)	Callis	1990

Pinnel Lock (No.26)	Callis	1990
Hollins Lock (No.27)	Callis	1989
Travis Mill Lock (No.28)	Callis	1989
Nip Square Lock (No.29)	Callis	1989
Winterbutlee Lock (No.30)	Callis	1988
Lightbank Lock (No.31)	Callis	1988
Sands Lock (No.32)	Callis	1988
Bottomley Lock (No.33)	Callis	1987
Warland Lower Lock (No.34)	Callis	1987
Warland Upper Lock (No.35)	Callis	1985
Warland Swing Bridge	New bridge – Rochdale MBC	1989
Longlees Lock (No.36)	Rochdale Canal Society volunteers	1980
Summit Pound	Extensive dredging and removal of toxic materials – Rochdale MBC	1992
West Summit Lock (No.37)	Rochdale MSC/Callis lock gates	1990
1st Lock below West Summit (No.38)	Rochdale MSC/Callis lock gates	1990
2nd Lock below West Summit (No.39)	Rochdale MSC/Callis lock gates	1990
Punchbowl Lock (No.40)	Rochdale MSC/Callis lock gates	1990
Fothergill & Harvey factory; office block and car park on line of canal.	Rochdale MBC Restoration of Lock No.41 (1st below Punchbowl) and Lock No.42 (2nd below Punchbowl) included as part of this project. Callis lock gates fitted:	1988
	Lock No.41	1989
	Lock No.42	1990

Thickone Lock (No.43)	Rochdale MSC/Callis lock gates	1990
Sladen Lock (No.44)	Rochdale MSC/Callis lock gates	1990
Pike House Lock (No.45)	Rochdale MSC/Callis lock gates	1990
Benthouse Lock (No.46)	Rochdale MSC/Callis lock gates	1990
Durn Lock (No.47)	Rochdale MSC/Callis lock gates	1991
Durn Bridge	New bridge – Rochdale MBC	1987
Littleborough Bottom Lock (No.48)	Rochdale MSC/Callis lock gates	1998
Ben Healey Bridge	New bridge – MP	2002
Smithy Bridge	New bridge – MP	2002
Little Clegg Footbridge	New bridge – Rochdale MBC	1999
Firgrove Bridge	New bridge – MP	2002
Deepdale Bridge	New bridge – MP	2002
Moss Upper Lock (No.49)	Rochdale MSC	1976
Moss Lower Lock (No.50)	Rochdale MSC	1976
Sealocrete narrowed section	MP	2002
Dicken Green Footbridge	New bridge – MP	2002
Hartley Green Bridge	New bridge – MP	2002
A627(M) Junction	New road layout built around new canal tunnel – MP	2002
Gorrels Way Bridge	New bridge – MP	2002
Bluepits Locks (Nos 51 and 52) M62 crossing	Part restored Rochdale MSC/MP New canal channel via existing subway under motorway;	2002

	Lock No.53 to north of motorway abandoned; new Lock No.53 built. – MP	2002
Slattocks or Laneside Locks (Nos 54–59)	Part restored Rochdale MSC/MP	2002
Irk Aqueduct	Leaks repaired – MP	2002
Boarshaw Lock (No.60)	Part restored Rochdale MSC/MP	2002
Scowcroft Lock (No.61)	Part restored Rochdale MSC/MP	2002
Coneygreen Lock (No.62)	Oldham MSC/Callis fitted Oldham built gates	1990
Walk Mill Lock (No.63)	Oldham MSC/ Callis fitted Oldham built gates	1990
Kay Lane Lock (No.64)	Oldham MSC/Callis fitted Oldham built gates	1990
Grimshaw Lane Bridge	New lifting bridge – MP	2002
Chadderton Broadway Business Park	Canal channel cleared etc. as part of redevelopment of former power station site including a new bridge across canal - Oldham MBC	1992
M60 motorway crossing.	Planned blockage of canal defeated following Public Inquiry. New canal channel and bridges built	1997
Failsworth Lock (No.65)	Oldham MSC/Callis	1990
Oldham Road Bridge	Infilled bridge arch re-established – Oldham MBC	1999
Failsworth shopping centre	Demolition of supermarket and construction of new canal through the site – MP	2002

Haweswater Aqueduct	Major water supply rerouted under canal – Oldham MBC	1999
Ashton Road West Bridge	New bridge – MP	2002
Poplar Street Bridge	New bridge – MP	2002
Tannersfield Locks (Nos 66–68)	Oldham MBC (Callis gates)	1999
Manchester shallowed section, including cascaded Locks Nos 69 (Newton Heath Lock), 70 (Pinfold Lock), 71 (Shears Lock), 72 (Scotchman's Lock), 73 (Ten Acres Lock), 74 (Drunken Bridge Lock), 75 (Slaters Higher Lock), 76 (Slaters Lower Lock), 77 (Anthony Lock), 78, 79 and 80 (Coalpit Locks) and 81 (Butler Lane Lock)	Canal channel and locks restored and rebuilt as necessary, new footbridges across canal – MP	2002
Ancoats Lane Lock (No.82)	Manchester City Council (Callis gates)	1999
Brownsfield Lock (No.83)	Manchester City Council (Callis gates)	2000

Beyond Brownsfield Lock, it is only a short distance to Ducie Street and the junction with the Ashton Canal. The 'Rochdale Nine' locks beyond, (Dale Street – No.84, Piccadilly – No.85, Chorlton Street – No.86, David Street – No.87, Oxford Road – No.88, Tib – No.89, Albion Mills – No.90, Tunnel – N0 91, and Duke's – No.92) leading to the Bridgewater Canal at Castlefield Basin were never officially abandoned. They were effectively impassable in the late 1960s and early 1970s until they were cleared and patched up by volunteers to reopen the Cheshire Ring of Canals.

BIBLIOGRAPHY

Archer, John H.G. (Edit), *Art and Architecture in Victorian Manchester* (Manchester University Press 1985). ISBN 0 7190 0957 X

Bolton, David, *Race Against Time* (Methuen, 1990). ISBN 0 7493 0994-6

Burnett, John, *A History of the Cost of Living* (Pelican, 1969)

Burton, Anthony, *The Great Days of the Canals* (David & Charles, 1989; Tiger Books International, 1995). ISBN 1 85501 695 8

Calder Navigation Society, *West Yorkshire Waterways Guide* (Calder Navigation Society, Fifth Edition, 1992). ISBN 0 9512400 13

Cumberlidge, Jane, *Inland Waterways of Great Britain (Seventh Edition)* (Imray Laurie Norie & Wilson, 1998). ISBN 0 85288 355 2

Gibson, Keith, *Pennine Dreams – the story of the Huddersfield Narrow Canal* (Tempus, 2002). ISBN 0 7524 2751 2

Giles, Colum, *Rural Houses of West Yorkshire 1400-1830* (Royal Commission on the Historical Monuments of England & West Yorkshire Metropolitan County Council, 1986). ISBN 0 11 701194 0

Giles, Colum & Goodall, Ian H, *Yorkshire Textile Mills – the buildings of the Yorkshire Textile Industry 1770-1930* (Royal Commission on the Historical Monuments of England & West Yorkshire Archaeology Service, 1992). ISBN 0 11 300038 3

Greenwood, Michael T., *The Rochdale –- an Illustrated History of trans-Pennine Canal Traffic* (Michael T. Greenwood, 18 Helston Drive, Royton).

Hadfield, Charles and Biddle, Gordon, *The Canals of North West England, Volume 2* (David & Charles, 1970). ISBN 0 7153 4992 9

Hadfield, Charles and Skempton, A.W., *William Jessop, Engineer* (David & Charles, 1979).

Jenkins, D.T., *The West Riding Wool Textile Industry 1770-1835 – a Study of Fixed Capital Formation* (Pasold Research Fund, 1975). ISBN 0 903859 05 X

Jennings, Bernard (Edit) and Hebden Bridge WEA Local History Group, *Pennine Valley – a History of Upper Calderdale* (Smith Settle Ltd, 1992). ISBN 1 870071 94 8

Laybourne, Keith, *Britain on the Breadline – a Social and Political History of Britain between the Wars* (Alan Sutton, 1990). ISBN 0-86299-490-X

Lower, John, *The South Pennine Ring* (The Hallamshire Press, 1998). ISBN 1 874718 37 7

Owen, David, *Canals to Manchester* (Manchester University Press, 1977; Reprinted 1987). ISBN 0 7190 2631 8

Parry, Keith, *Trans-Pennine Heritage – Hills, People and Transport* (David & Charles, 1981). ISBN 0 7153 8019 2

Ransom, P.J.G, *The Archaeology of Canals* (World's Work, 1979)

Robertson, William, *A History of Rochdale, Past & Present* (William Robertson, Rochdale, 1875)

Robertson, William, *A Social & Political History of Rochdale* (William Robertson, Rochdale 1889)

Rolt, L.T.C., *Narrow Boat* (Eyre & Spottiswoode, 1944; Reprinted Budding Books, 1998). ISBN 1 84015 0645

Strong, Roy, *The Story of Britain – a People's History* (Pimlico, 1998). ISBN 0 7126 6546 3

Squires, Roger W, *Canals Revived – the Story of the Waterway Restoration Movement* (Moonraker Press, 1979). ISBN 0 239 00191 5

Squires, Roger W, *The New Navvies – a History of the Modern Waterways Restoration Movement* (Phillimore & Co Ltd, 1983). ISBN 0 85033 364 4

Williams, Mike with Fairnie D.A., *Cotton Mills in Greater Manchester* (The Greater Manchester Archaeological Unit with the Royal Commission on the Historical Monuments of England, Carnegie Publishing, 1992).

INDEX

If you are interested in purchasing
other books published by Tempus, or in case you have
difficulty finding any Tempus books in your local bookshop,
you can also place orders directly through our website

www.tempus-publishing.com